Colossians

Living in Christ

Bible Study/Commentary Series

Steve Copland

Colossians

Living in Christ: Bible Study/commentary Series

Published by Steve Copland at Createspace

Steve Copland is a self-supported missionary from New Zealand, serving The Lord in Ukraine since 2003. He is a member of the pastoral team at New Life evangelical church in Kiev and former lecturer at the Ukraine Evangelical Seminary and International Christian University.

Contents

Introduction

Whenever we study one of the New Testament epistles (letters) it is important that we firstly ask some questions. Where was the city situated? Who wrote the letter to the Church there? Why was the letter initially written to this Church? These questions are vital for understanding the context of the letter, without which we may be misinterpreting or laying our own ideas onto the text. It is also important to understand how the culture which received the letter was different to our own. We will do this as we study Colossians and apply the lessons God has for us in this 21st century?

I. Where?

The city of Colossae was situated near the towns of Hierapolis and Laodicea in the valley of Lycus in what is now Turkey. It was not a particularly important city, rather one you would travel through on your way to somewhere else. It is most likely that Paul never visited this city in his life-time. The Church in Colossae was apparently founded by Epaphras (1:7).

II. Who?

Like so many of the New Testament letters, Colossians was written by the apostle Paul. He was in prison at Rome when he wrote the letter, and it was written about the same time as he wrote the letter to the Ephesians. Colossians was written after Paul received a report from Epaphras concerning a heresy which had surfaced and was threatening the true teaching of the gospel in Colossae. There were several Churches around and near Colossae who were also practising these heretical teachings, so Paul wrote Colossians to an entire area, rather than to only one group. In 4:16 he asks that this letter be read in the church at Laodicea and that the Colossians read one from Laodicea. If Paul wrote a special letter to the Laodicean church, it has been lost to us.

III. What?

What was the heresy? The heresy confronted at Colossae was an early form of Gnosticism, a heresy which swept through the Church for over 100 years and seriously threatened the purity of the gospel message. The book of 1st John was specifically written to combat Gnosticism.

Here is an exert from my book *Religion: History and Mystery* which explains this heresy.

The Book of Acts, chapter 8, records the meeting of Simon Peter, an apostle of Christ, and Simon Magus who was considered to be a sorcerer. After seeing that people received the Holy Spirit after the apostles laid hands upon them, Magus tried to purchase this power with money. Simon Magus had taken an interest in Christian theology but was never converted. According to tradition, he became the father of Gnosticism. Keep in mind that Simon Magus was a Samaritan by birth. His mother was a Jewess and father Persian. There was a great deal of animosity between Jew and Samaritan, and perhaps this led Simon to seek other answers to life rather than within the pages of his mother's religion of Judaism.

Gnosticism comes from the word 'gnosis', or knowledge, and in this case, a secret knowledge available to only a select group. Gnostics believed that there was an uncreated god/goddess who created several Aeons, one known as Sophia (Greek for wisdom). Sophia, in turn, created demigods. One of the demigods was the Hebrew God Jehovah. According to the Gnostics, Jehovah created the universe and all material things, but, because he was a jealous god, he was responsible for evil in the world. Jehovah tried to stop the first humans from receiving knowledge. After they tried to gain knowledge by eating of the 'Tree of the Knowledge of Good and Evil', Jehovah banned them from the Garden of Eden and punished them.

Lucifer is the good guy in Gnostic teaching; he had crept into the garden to help the humans find gnosis (knowledge) and was then cursed by Jehovah. Sophia sent Lucifer's brother, Jesus, to teach people how to get back to the truth, but His disciples misunderstood Him. Gnostics believed that the entire material world was evil because it had been created by a lesser god, Jehovah. Therefore, they claimed that Jesus never had a real human body at all; He simply appeared to be human. This particular idea is called 'Docetism', from the word *doce*, 'to appear'. For Christians, this theology, apart from being offensive, reduced the gospel message to a farce. Moreover, if Jesus wasn't a real person, then His sacrifice on the cross was not real, and therefore, ineffective. In his first letter to the Church the apostle John writes against Gnosticism, putting an emphasis on the real humanity of Jesus.

For Gnostics, only the spirit world can be pure and holy, taking its roots back to Sophia who has no material form. For the leaders of Gnosticism, such as Simon Magus, the power to perform the supernatural was given to those who climbed up through various stages of esoteric teaching, and was closely tied to visitations of angels and other spiritual beings.

IV. Gnostic Practices

Little is known about Gnostic practices as much of their literature was destroyed. However, some of the 'gospels' written by Gnostics to counter the Christian gospels still survive, and also a lot of literature written by Christians, such as Irenaeus, about their practices. Salvation for Gnostics is to find the spark of the divine Sophia which remains within and develop it through various techniques, including meditation and asceticism. Many scholars have seen a very direct link to Eastern religions here, especially some of the early teachings in the Gathas and Avestas, the writings of the Zoroastrians. This would not be unlikely as Simon Magus' father was Persian and may have had access to such literature.

Women played a large role in leadership, especially because of their communication with spirits and angels (Col: 2:18) who presumably passed on secret information about salvation. Within Gnosticism there is a great emphasis on the human person as divine and self development to full divinity. Self is essentially good because humans can become divine, and many Gnostic practices resemble closely the religions of the Aryans such as Hinduism and Buddhism.

From the writings which have survived, it appears that Gnosticism split into two radically different factions. On the one side were the ascetics who taught that the body must be overcome and restrained. Strict forms of self-discipline were applied in order to gain higher spiritual awareness, a practice Paul mentions in Colossians 2:23.

On the other side was almost the complete opposite. Some Gnostics believed that the body could not affect the spirit at all and practiced extremely liberal forms of sexuality, indulging in orgies. They believed that the emotions, lusts, and desires must be released in order to free the spirit from bodily bondage, in a similar way to the people of the past who had worshipped Baal, Ashtorah, etc. In general terms, anything that Jehovah banned must be the way to spiritual freedom. Jehovah had destroyed the cities of Sodom and Gomorrah for their immoral sexuality and homosexuality, so it was assumed that similar practices must be beneficial in finding secret knowledge.

V. Points as they relate to the Colossians

The first point of Gnosticism separates people into groups, those with special knowledge and those without it. In Colossae, the claim was that this special knowledge was being given by angels, and angels were being worshipped as a result of this teaching. As no angel of God would ever accept worship, we can safely assume that it was fallen angels (demons) which were being worshipped and giving these people false experiences of 'knowledge'.

The second point is even more of a problem. If all matter is evil, then how could a good God create such evil? Also, the Gnostics claimed that God could never become truly human because He would have to touch the physical/evil creation, and they believed that this was impossible. The Gnostics taught that there were levels of holiness, and many beings with less and less divinity until we get to Jesus and the angels.

VI. Paul's Answer

In Colossians Paul points out that every believer has received the Divine knowledge through Jesus Christ, and that the Holy Spirit dwells in all Christians, not just a chosen few with 'special' knowledge. Paul also reminds them that Christ is the Creator of all things; therefore, the physical universe is not evil. He tells them that using extreme physical discipline has no value for holiness, neither

7

should they worship angels, nor think they are holy for keeping human based rules and traditions. He reminds them not to be involved in sexual immorality and gives them some practical advice for Christian living.

The letter to Colossae has many beautiful points, especially about the person of Jesus Christ in chapter one. It is a book which I believe is very useful in all cultures, especially in cultures where religious and spiritual traditions have become superstitions. Here in Ukraine, where I minister, the 'worship' of saints and angels is a common practise among many who consider themselves 'Orthodox'. In Western cultures some churches have allowed eastern religious practices into the Church, and there are many leaders claiming to have special powers from the Holy Spirit which I consider very Gnostic. We will discuss these further as we study this book.

There is also a lot of practical advice for marriage, bringing up children, living in the Spirit, Christian witness, and relationships. All of these we will study while keeping in mind the cultural differences we have with the original readers.

Study One

The Great Trilogy: Faith, Love and Hope

Colossians 1: 3-8

1 Paul, an apostle of Christ Jesus by the will of God, and Timothy our brother ,² To God's holy people in Colossae, the faithful brothers and sisters in Christ: Grace and peace to you from God our Father.
³ We always thank God, the Father of our Lord Jesus Christ, when we pray for you, ⁴ because we have heard of your faith in Christ Jesus and of the love you have for all God's people— ⁵ the faith and love that spring from the hope stored up for you in heaven and about which you have already heard in the true message of the gospel ⁶ that has come to you. In the same way, the gospel is bearing fruit and growing throughout the whole world—just as it has been doing among you since the day you heard it and truly understood God's grace. ⁷ You learned it from Epaphras, our dear fellow servant, who is a faithful minister of Christ on our behalf, ⁸ and who also told us of your love in the Spirit.

Paul is in prison. The year is 62 AD. He has never been to this city of Colossae. An evangelist called Epaphras, who has reported everything about the church to Paul, planted this congregation. The letter also introduces Timothy who is staying with Paul in Rome at this time. Paul tells them that he and Timothy thank the Lord for three things.

1. The faith they have in Christ Jesus.
2. The love they have for all of the saints.
3. The hope they have stored up for themselves in heaven.

These three are the essence of Christianity: Faith, love and hope. Faith looks upward to God, love looks outward to others, and hope looks forward to the future. Faith rests on the past work of Christ, love

9

works in the present, and hope anticipates the future. These are the great trilogy of Christianity.

I. Faith

Faith could be defined as the soul looking up to God.

Hebrews 11:1 states it this way; *'Now faith is being sure of what we hope for and certain of what we do not see'*.

In the original language of Hebrews the meaning of faith is a deeply philosophical one, especially regarding the ideas of hope and certainty. The idea expressed is that what we do not see is the underlying basis of all that is real and tangible. In other words, faith is built on a conviction, a knowing that God is the foundation of everything we believe. Our 'hope', is not like a child hoping to get a particular present for his/her birthday, but rather a deep conviction, a certainty, because God is certain.

Faith is the thing we put our trust in, that which we rely upon. Our faith is built on certain facts, but facts are not enough. Facts give us a basis to trust, but trust is a decision of the soul. Faith is saying, 'I believe that my Creator loves me, that His promises are true, and that He is the only absolute certainty in this life and the next'. Faith hears the words, the promises of God, and then acts on those promises. Faith, then, stands upon a conviction, a revelation which must always be confirmed by Scripture, and then acts upon that conviction. Without the action of trusting, there is no faith, merely dead knowledge.

Let's look at an example from Luke 6:46-49.

'Why do you call me, 'Lord, Lord' and not do what I say? I will show you what he is like who comes to me and hears my words and puts them into practice. He is like a man building a house, who dug down deep and laid the foundation on rock. When a flood came, the torrent struck that house but could not shake it, because it was well built. But the one who hears my words and does not put them into practice is like a man who built a house on the ground without a foundation. The moment the torrent struck that house, it collapsed and its destruction was complete.'

10

In this well-known parable the Lord calls us to *hear* His words and *practice* them. His words are the facts, the promises. That is His part, and ours is to act, to trust Him in every area of our lives. Sometimes it will be difficult, sometimes it will seem almost impossible. These are the storms of life. Jesus mentions a great flood, the power of the water completely beyond human control. The life built on Jesus Christ will not even be shaken; it will stand under the power of the water.

But if we hear Jesus words and refuse to practice them, when the flood comes, as it does to all people, our lives will be like a house which collapses into rubble and is completely destroyed. Jesus' words are also a warning about final destruction at the judgment. No person can escape the floods of this life; every one of us will be in situations which are out of our control. But Jesus Christ is the Creator, the One who protects us from the storm.

Jesus' question is incredibly important. "Why do you call me, 'Lord, Lord,' and do not do what I say?" That's the challenge for every one of us. If our faith is real faith, the proof is in our doing as He says, in trusting Him with our lives.

II. Love

Love looks outward to others. Paul says in verse 5 that 'faith and love spring from the hope we have that is stored up in heaven'. Love, then, is the outward fruit of those who have faith and hope. Paul writes about love in 1st Corinthians 13. He is writing to Christians who thought they were very spiritual because of their spiritual gifts, but, at the same time they were arguing and fighting among themselves. In other words, they were not exercising love. Paul tells them that no matter what great deeds they do, if those deeds are not done in love, they are eternally useless.

The Greek word 'love' that Paul uses is 'agape'. In 1st John 4:16 it says 'God is love', the same word, 'agape'. Therefore, we could replace the word 'love' in Corinthians 13 with 'God'.

'God is patient, God is kind. He does not envy, He does not boast, He is not proud. He is not rude, is not self-seeking, is not easily

angered, He keeps no record of wrongs. God does not delight in evil but rejoices with the truth, etc.'

Without the love of God within us, motivating our actions, our actions are not actions of love done in faith. There are many people who do good things, have a great amount of knowledge, can give everything they have to the poor, and are even willing to die for what they believe, all actions which Paul describes, but if they don't have 'agape love', if they don't have God, everything they did was eternally useless.

We are called to love each other, not just a *feeling* of love, but putting each other before ourselves. Agape love is an action which often requires self-sacrifice. God Himself set down this precedent for 'God so loved the world that He gave His only begotten Son' (John 3:16). We are called to act in love towards others, just as God acted in love towards us.

1st John 4: 7-21.

[17] This is how love is made complete among us so that we will have confidence on the Day of Judgment: In this world we are like Jesus. [18] There is no fear in love. But perfect love drives out fear, because fear has to do with punishment. The one who fears is not made perfect in love.

[19] We love because he first loved us. [20] Whoever claims to love God yet hates a brother or sister is a liar. For whoever does not love their brother and sister, whom they have seen, cannot love God, whom they have not seen. [21] And he has given us this command: Anyone who loves God must also love their brother and sister.

When we are in Christ we have no need to fear judgement because God's love has been made perfect in us. However, we are called to manifest this same love outwardly to others, just as God acted in love towards us.

III. Hope

Hope looks forward to the future. Paul said our faith and love spring from the hope we have stored up for us in heaven. What do we have stored up for us? John 14:1-4;

"Do not let your hearts be troubled. You believe in God; believe also in me. ² My Father's house has many rooms; if that were not so, would I have told you that I am going there to prepare a place for you? ³ And if I go and prepare a place for you, I will come back and take you to be with me that you also may be where I am. ⁴ You know the way to the place where I am going."

Jesus asks us to trust in Him, and then tells us He is going back to heaven to prepare a place for us so that we can be with Him. Do you believe this? In 1st Peter 1:3-5 the apostle calls this a 'living hope' and speaks of our inheritance. He says that it can 'never perish (be destroyed), spoil, or fade, and it is kept in heaven for us'. The word 'kept' means a garrison or keep, a fortress. Peter's analogy is that Jesus Christ Himself is guarding our inheritance. While we wait for it, we are also shielded by our faith and God's power. This is our hope. It isn't an uncertain hope like the child who hopes he will get a particular present at Christmas. This inheritance of ours has been promised by the Lord Himself, the One who never lies, the One whose promises can be trusted. The Bible says that we are heirs, and co-heirs with Christ (Romans 8:17). That means that all that belongs to Christ belongs to us.

What will heaven be like? I don't know, but I've always liked the words of Keith Green, a Christian singer who died in a plane crash with his son some years ago. Keith said this. "The Lord spent 6 days creating this world, but He's been preparing our home for 2000 years". Do you have hope in the promises of Jesus, that He is preparing a place for you? Are you excited about that? And does this hope make faith and love spring from you?

In the next three verses (6-8) Paul summarizes his opening remarks about the gospel of faith, hope and love. He says it is producing fruit all over the world and growing as it should.

Faith, love and hope are the great trilogy. Faith looks upwards towards the Lord, trusting in Him, letting Him build the house on the rock against the storms of life. Agape love looks outwards to others and is the natural expression of those who are born again. This kind of love is only available to those who know Christ, those who are filled with His agape love. And hope looks forward to the future, and lives for that future. We know that whatever happens to us, we have an inheritance waiting for us which is infinitely more incredible than anything we can have or imagine in this life.

Study Two

Knowing God's Will

Colossians 1:9

In this second part of the opening remarks of his letter, Paul tells the Colossian what he prays for them.

'For this reason, since the day we heard about you, we have not stopped praying for you and asking God to fill you with the knowledge of his will through all spiritual wisdom and understanding'.

The first thing he prays for is that they will be filled with 'the knowledge of God's will'. In this study we will examine in brief what Scripture says about how we can know the will of God for our lives. Why does Paul mention this first? For two reasons! This letter is written against Gnosticism which is about 'knowledge', so Paul is praying that they have the most important knowledge. Also, we cannot accomplish God's will unless we know what it is. The whole of the Christian life is about doing the will of God. Jesus stressed this continually in His teachings, so it is vital that we understand. Consider this verse from Matthew 7: 2.

21 "Not everyone who says to me, 'Lord, Lord,' will enter the kingdom of heaven, but only the one who does the will of my Father who is in heaven. Matthew 7: 21

I. God's General Will

We may speak of God's will as general and individual. God's general will is that which we find outlined in Scripture. Scripture is full of warnings, encouragements, commands, advice and so on. Every major topic concerning our salvation, sanctification, being filled with the Holy Spirit, living in loving relationships, repentance, and so on, is on every page we read. God's general will for all of us is non-negotiable, and we can fill our hearts with this knowledge through the daily reading of His word.

II. God's Will for Individuals

But what about His will for us as individuals? This is often more difficult for us to know. We all have questions such as: Who should I marry, which university should I attend, what do you want me to do in the future Lord, are you calling me into full-time ministry, how do I win my friends and family to the gospel? Most of us would be thankful if the Lord just sent us an e-mail, but that would not be 'walking by faith' or being 'led by the Spirit'. Everything in our Christian life must be by faith because 'without faith it is impossible to please God' (Hebrews 11:6). I believe that the Lord wants us to know the answers to all of these personal questions, in His time, because in my reading of Scripture He always tells people His will before commanding them to act in faith. He doesn't often give them the outcome, but He always lights that first step.

There are some who teach that God doesn't tell us His will for us as individuals. I once heard a pastor giving young people advice on who to marry. He told them to look for a list of godly characteristics and 'go for it'. One person asked if God wanted to be involved in the choosing process and the pastor's reply was 'there is no mandate for that in the Bible'. I would disagree entirely. God chose Isaac's wife (Genesis 24). The issue is not that the Lord isn't interested in telling us who to marry, or what university to attend, or any other important question; the problem is people are too afraid to ask or trust Him in these decisions.

III. Conditions for Knowing God's Will

This raises the very first condition for knowing God's will. If we have already decided what we are going to do, despite what the Lord says, we will never hear His voice; never know His will concerning that thing. The first condition to knowing God's will is to come to Him with open hands asking Him to take out or put in whatever is His will for us. If we can do this sincerely, in the same way we should have done when we were born again, then we will be practicing 'taking up

16

our cross daily' (Luke 9:23) and He will give us the knowledge of His will. But there are several other conditions to knowing God's will. They are found in Romans 12:1-2.

'Therefore, I urge you, brothers, in view of God's mercy, to offer your bodies as living sacrifices, holy and pleasing to God - which is your spiritual worship. Do not conform any longer to the pattern of this world, but be transformed by the renewing of your mind. Then you will be able to test and approve what God's will is - his good, pleasing and perfect will'.

1. Offer our bodies as living sacrifices, holy and pleasing.
2. Do not conform to the world.
3. Be transformed by the renewing of our minds.

'Holy and Pleasing'.

Paul's appeal in Romans 12:1-2 abolishes any idea that we can live immorally in our bodies and deceive ourselves that this does not affect our 'spiritual worship'. Holiness implies sanctification, the action of 'being made holy' (Hebrews 10:14). The Holy Spirit dwelling within every believer works to empower us to holy living, our part is to be 'led by the Spirit' (Galatians 5:16ff).

The offering of our bodies also implies other powerful and positive aspects. We can use our bodies for various forms of service. Every day we make intellectual decisions as to how we can use our bodies to worship God. In an emotional sense we can lift our hands to express what we feel in our hearts, or we can dance, bow down, etc. All of these are emotional responses, but Paul appeals to us on an intellectual level in this verse. He calls us to practical worship. Jesus offered his body in practical service and we are called to do the same. It is about serving Christ even when we don't *feel* like serving Christ.

'Do not Conform...to the pattern of this World'.

The 'world' Paul is speaking of is not the natural creation, but rather the 'market place' mentality that tells us to live for our bodily pleasures rather than for the sanctification of our souls. Scripture

17

warns us many times about loving the market place mentality or system of the world. Read for example 1st John 2: 15-17, and James 4:4-5.

The word 'conformed' means to be moulded; fitted into a mould through a process of imitation. Don't let the world shape you into its mould any longer. The idea here is that the world tries to force everyone into its pattern of thinking, its way of life, and people become world shaped through imitating the world's example. Consider that two of the most powerful forces which we are moulded into are our traditions and cultures. Our traditions and cultures are made up of those things which our predecessors imitated from their parents, and may often be contrary to Scriptural teachings. When we give our lives to Christ we agree to follow Him exclusively, and this includes giving up everything in our cultures and traditions which do not glorify him.

What are some of the traditions and cultural practices of people in your country which are contrary to Scripture?

'But be Transformed'.

The second part of Paul's appeal is to be transformed by the 'renewing of our minds'. The Greek verb Paul uses is '*metamorphoo*', from which we take the English word 'metamorphous'. This means to change from one thing into another thing. This word is used to describe when a caterpillar becomes a butterfly. It is also used to describe what happened to Jesus in Matthew 17: 2 on the mountain where he was 'transfigured'. Many commentators believe that what the disciples witnessed in Jesus is very similar, or even exactly the same, to what happens to us at the rapture, or when we leave this body.

For the Christian, being transformed is the gradual process of becoming like Christ as Paul says in 2nd Corinthians 3:18.

[18] And we all, who with unveiled faces contemplate the Lord's glory, are being transformed into his image with ever-increasing glory, which comes from the Lord, who is the Spirit.

Notice here that Paul says that this transformation '*comes from the Lord, who is the Spirit.*' It is the Holy Spirit dwelling within us who does the work of transformation. Our part is obedience. Within the

18

born again believer are two natures, a sinful nature which we inherited, and a Divine Nature which was gifted to us at conversion. We have two choices. We can allow the Holy Spirit to transform us into the likeness of Christ, or we can live according to the desires of our sinful nature. If we choose the latter, then the Scriptures suggest that at best we are a disobedient Christian, who will lose our reward in heaven, and at worst we may not be born again at all. We have the power within us, through the Holy Spirit, to live according to God's will, but we are not robots, we have a choice.

In Ephesians 4:22-24 Paul uses the idea of changing a piece of clothing to describe this process.

22 You were taught, with regard to your former way of life, to put off your old self, which is being corrupted by its deceitful desires; 23 to be made new in the attitude of your minds; 24 and to put on the new self, created to be like God in true righteousness and holiness.

We are to take off the old self and put on the new. In Luke 9:23 Jesus says that we must "take up our cross daily". Again this is denial of self, a denial of that sin nature which wants to dominate our thinking and actions. All of these analogies, symbols and ideas come down to the same thing. The Holy Spirit within us is continually transforming us into the likeness of Christ as we walk in the Spirit. Every day the Spirit guides and directs us about how to live. We hear his voice helping us to make decisions about almost every area of life. But His voice is soft, He doesn't scream in our ear. We can choose to ignore Him, and we all do this on occasions. We have many old habits which dominate our thinking patterns and these take time to change. We have the powerful influences of tradition and culture, and we must discern what is right and wrong in these areas. But if we are really honest with ourselves, we are seldom confused about how we should live, especially in the day to day areas of life.

Paul tells us that if we apply these conditions to our lives, with the help and guidance of the Holy Spirit, then we will be able to 'test and approve' God's will. It is worth saying again that we must seek His will with open hands, 'taking up our cross daily', otherwise, we are merely waiting to hear what we want to hear. However, if we are meeting the criteria set out above, there are some ways in which we

19

can 'test and approve' His will. Keep in mind that the Lord always wants us to know His will and will always lead by His Spirit.

IV. Testing and Approving God's Will

What are some of the methods we can use for 'testing and approving' God's will?

1. Tell the Lord about how you are feeling and be reading the word, praying, and listening to His voice. He may put into your mind the methods to test and approve that you should use. He will most likely also speak through the Scriptures. He never contradicts the Scriptures.

2. I see no problem in putting out a 'fleece' as Gideon did.

3. Listen to the advice of other Christians, and ask the Lord to confirm His will through them, especially through leaders or people you know are walking in step with the Spirit.

4. Ask Him to close every door which He doesn't want you to step through, and be willing to step through any door He opens.

5. Be very careful that you are not manipulating signs to fit your own desires. Remember that the first criteria for knowing God's will is to have a willingness to say "Yes Lord" to whatever He asks.

6. Don't be content with only one of these things, but use a combination of things. Remember that the Lord wants us to be absolutely sure of His will so that we can act accordingly. He will not leave us ignorant, so always expect to get an answer.

7. WAIT. Don't rush into things. The Lord's timing is always perfect so don't be impatient. If you don't get an immediate answer from the Lord it's because there are other factors or people involved and He is sorting out all of the details. Trust Him, for He is trustworthy. Expect an answer, expect to be led and you will be led.

Paul's prayer was for God to fill us with the knowledge of His will through all spiritual wisdom and understanding. If we are coming to the Lord with open hands, daily taking up our cross, offering our bodies as living sacrifices, and allowing His transforming process rather than conforming to this world, then Paul's prayer will be answered in our lives.

Study Three

Paul's Prayer

Colossians 1:10-14

In this passage of Scripture Paul outlines the content of his prayer for the Colossians.

'And we pray this in order that you may live a life worthy of the Lord and may please him in every way: bearing fruit in every good work, growing in the knowledge of God, (11) being strengthened with all power according to his glorious might so that you may have great endurance and patience, and joyfully (12) giving thanks to the Father, who has qualified you to share in the inheritance of the saints in the kingdom of light. (13) For he has rescued us from the dominion of darkness and brought us into the kingdom of the Son he loves, (14) in whom we have redemption, the forgiveness of sins.'

This prayer brings out an interesting progression. In verse 9, as we saw in the last study, Paul prays that they might know God's will, and then he adds this phrase, 'through all spiritual wisdom and understanding'. This phrase is linked to the heresies which are infiltrating the Church in Colossae. Knowing God's will and having spiritual wisdom go hand in hand. Once we are aware of God's will, then it is time for action. As I implied in the last study, God doesn't want us to act presumptuously, as this can lead to many errors, however, once He has made His will clear to us we need to act, for this is the outworking of faith. Now let's observe the progression of Christian maturity in Paul's prayer.

And we pray this in order that you may live a life worthy of the Lord and may please him in every way: bearing fruit in every good work, growing in the knowledge of God...

22

The knowledge of God's will leads to living a life worthy of the Lord which pleases Him in every way. This kind of life produces fruit in every good work. There are fruits of the Spirit and fruits of good works. We use the fruits of the Spirit to do good works, and when we do good works we likewise produce the fruits of the Spirit. These good works are service to others, both in Christ and unsaved.

Contrary to what some teach and believe, good works are not something we do to maintain our salvation. Salvation is solely the work of Jesus Christ:

'for it is by grace you have been saved through faith - and this is not from your selves, it is the gift of God - not by works, so that no one can boast' (Ephesians 2:8-9).

Jesus Christ is both the author and perfector of our faith (Hebrews 12:2), and no person can ever take any credit for attributing to their salvation. Such an idea is considered a form of 'slander' and blasphemy towards Christ, as it nullifies His selfless sacrifice on the cross. This form of slander has existed from the very birth of the Church. In those early days there were many Jews claiming to be Christians who were insisting that Christian converts must keep the law of Moses in order to be saved (Acts 15:1). Their error came from a heart of pride, a belief that all Jews were saved and all Gentiles were simply 'Gentile sinners' (Galatians 2:15). They believed that doing works of the law saved them, and were deeply surprised at Paul's teaching that all were sinners before God.

In these days in which we live there are groups who have resurrected this old heresy, and just as many that believe a Christian can lose their salvation. The latter then teach that good works are needed to keep a person's name from being deleted from the Book of Life. This topic deserves a study on its own and we will address it when we examine 1:23.

'...bearing fruit in every good work, growing in the knowledge of God...'

As we produce these fruits we also grow in our knowledge of God. When we are growing in the fruits of the Spirit; love, joy, peace, patience, self-control, etc., we grow in our knowledge of God, for all of these reflect His character. Also, when we are serving Christ in the Church, and in evangelism, we grow in the knowledge of God's love for his bride the Church, and in his heart for the lost.

'...being strengthened with all power according to his glorious might so that you may have great endurance and patience...,

Now Paul links God's power with our knowledge of Him. Notice how Peter does the same thing in his second letter. 2nd Peter 1:3,

'His divine power has given us everything we need for life and godliness through our knowledge of him who called us by his own glory and goodness.'

God calls us to live lives which are worthy of Him, producing fruit in every good work; producing a godly character and wining souls. By ourselves these things are completely impossible, so He has firstly given us His Divine power within us, and as we do His will, we are constantly strengthened by that power. Some people feel that they haven't experienced that power. Often it is because they have not put themselves in the position of needing it. Consider this analogy.

A soldier goes to a camp and trains for war. He learns military disciplines, obedience etc. He learns what he must do when in different combat situations through many drills and exercises which attempt to simulate battle conditions. He learns how to use his weapons; guns, knives, hand-grenades, etc. Then he goes home. At home he is the same old citizen with a lot of head-knowledge and training. However, if he goes to war he suddenly has other elements which were not present in training camp. He has fear, adrenalin, he has an enemy trying to stop him and kill him. This situation requires him to call upon every element of strength, and to daily renew that strength.

Those who go to battle for God, which is in effect to do His will, serving others, evangelizing, and living a life worthy of the gospel, will need God's power every day, will need to be strengthened by the filling of the Holy Spirit every day. This will produce great endurance and patience in them, as Paul says in verse 11, and they will also have good reason to give thanks joyfully.

'...giving thanks to the Father, who has qualified us to share in the inheritance of the saints in the kingdom of light. For he has rescued us from the dominion of darkness and brought us into the kingdom of the Son he loves, in whom we have redemption, the forgiveness of sins'.

If we can read these promises of God without desiring to 'give thanks joyfully', then I wonder if we have any inkling of what we have been saved from, what has been done for us, and what is prepared for us. We are 'qualified to share in the inheritance of the saints in the kingdom of light'. Paul tells us we are 'co-heirs with Christ', (Romans 8:17) meaning that all that is His is also ours. We have been rescued out of the 'dominion of darkness'. Notice the word 'dominion' here as opposed to Christ's 'kingdom'. The word dominion comes from the idea of being dominated as a slave under a dictator. Satan is that dictator, the one who 'blinds the minds of the unbelieving' (2 Corinthians 4:4). Satan is the prince of darkness, and those who have not accepted and embraced God's offer of rescue, will eventually be cast into eternal darkness (Matthew 22:13).

But Christ *'reveals the deep things of darkness and brings deep shadows into the light'* (Job 12:22), because *'the people walking in darkness have seen a great light; on those living in the land of shadow of death a light has dawned'* (Isaiah 9:2).

We who know Christ were once under Satan's dominion, walking in darkness, unable to rescue ourselves. But we have been rescued by Jesus Christ, the 'Light of the World' and our inheritance is with Him in the kingdom of light. He calls us to walk in the light as He is in the light (1st John 2:6), living a life worthy of Him and bearing fruit in every good work, reflecting His glory as we 'let our light shine before men, that they may see our good deeds and praise our Father in heaven' (Matthew 5:16). In order to do this He strengthens us 'with all power according to His glorious might' so that we may stand against all the schemes of the enemy (Ephesians 6: 10-11).

There are times when we are watching the news and see horrific scenes of violence, cruelty, immorality, greed, death, disease and corruption, that these verses we have read remind us of this dark world in which we live. But there are as many times when we are enjoying times with friends and family, looking forward to some important event; marriage, a new car, our first home, holidaying in the mountains or at a beach, playing sports, etc. The world often seems like a pretty nice place. At such times it is often difficult to see the intensity of this dominion of darkness because all seems well in our little corner of the world. We may have close friends and family who are simply uninterested in Christianity, friends who are helpful, loving and supportive. Do we view such people as 'walking in darkness', blinded by the 'god of this world', in need of rescue from eternal separation from our Lord? We should, we must, for this is the reality.

There are many decent unbelievers in this world, people who are basically law-abiding citizens. They may be war heroes, or volunteers involved in charity work, they are people who you could never imagine committing murder, stealing, cheating on their spouse or abusing children, indeed they are people you may have a great deal of respect for. But the truth is, all of us are sinners, all have rebelled against our Creator, and all, under vile circumstances, can and do things which come out of our fallen natures. Unbelieving people are still 'nice people' by the grace, provision, and love of God. Satan usually leaves such people alone, for the most part, as he knows that pushing them to the edge of despair may push them into the arms of Jesus Christ as easily as pushing them to hate God.

Be a person that 'bears fruit in every good work', a person who acts with all 'spiritual wisdom and understanding', a person who bears witness to the glorious power of God when difficult times come and we need 'great endurance and patience'. In those difficult times, which all families go through, we can be the 'light of the world'. Be prayerful and patient, and above all, thankful to the one who has rescued us, made us 'saints', and given us an inheritance with Him in His glorious kingdom of light.

Study Four

Who is Jesus Christ? (Part One)

Colossians 1:15-17

(15) 'For he is the image of the invisible God, the firstborn over all creation. (16) For by him all things were created: things in heaven and on earth, visible and invisible, whether thrones or powers or rulers or authorities; all things were created by him and for him. (17) He is before all things, and in him all things hold together'.

Throughout the world there is a lot of confusion about who Jesus Christ is. Much of that confusion stems from the fact that people refuse to believe something which cannot be intellectually understood, namely, that God is triune. The doctrine of the Trinity, although never expressed in those words, is present within the pages of Scripture. It defies mathematical logic, defies definitions and analogies, although many have tried, for the Creator exists primarily outside of this created world. Therefore, many people such as the Jehovah's Witnesses and Mormons, like the Pharisees of the first century, and Arians in the third, refuse to believe that God is Triune by nature.

From the beginning of man's fall, and separation from God, we have created our own gods and idols. These were all gods which could be understood intellectually; weather gods, fertility gods etc. But has any human being ever tried to create a god that was impossible to understand, one that was intellectually indefinable? Only God could do such a thing. I have often been asked by Jehovah's Witnesses, and others, if I understand the doctrine of the Trinity. I always say 'no'! 'How, then, can you believe in such a thing', they ask. 'Because no man could ever conceive such an idea', is my reply, 'but more than this, because the Scriptures declare this truth, and Jesus Christ has made it known in history, and to me personally'.

These three verses we are about to study are some of the most profound ever written. Some scholars believe they may have been part

27

of an early hymn, but whatever the case, they are the foundation of all that Paul has to say in the rest of his letter, and the first part of his answer to the question 'who is Jesus Christ?' Throughout his letter Paul will draw our attention to Jesus Christ as God and man, for both are equally important for our salvation. In this study we will examine His Deity, and in the next His humanity.

Firstly, Paul writes that He is the 'image of the invisible God'. Our English word 'image' may suggest a copy, something less than perfect, but the Greek text means something closer to 'revelation'. Jesus Christ is the physical manifestation of God, the Father who is invisible to human eyes. John tells us that *'no one has ever seen God, but God the only Son, who is at the Father's side, has made him known'* (John 1:18), and Jesus Himself stated *'anyone who has seen me has seen the Father'* (John 14:9). The writer to the Hebrews (1:3) puts it this way, *'The Son is the radiance of God's glory and the exact representation of his being, sustaining all things by his powerful word'*.

These words are very clear, but the facts which they state are impossible for us to comprehend. How can someone who created this incredible universe with all of its complexity, infinite detail and perfect design, then become small enough to be a part of it? Paul would answer such a question by referring to Christ as the *'mystery which has been kept hidden for ages and generations, but is now disclosed to the saints'* (Colossians 1:26).

Paul calls Him the 'firstborn of all creation' (*prototokos pases ktiseos*). This term 'firstborn' (*protokos*) has several meanings. The Jehovah's Witnesses claim that this phrase proves that Jesus was the first created being. They are absolutely wrong. In Greek the phrase literally means 'begotten before all creation'. This word does not mean to be created; rather, it means to exist eternally in a physical form. This term is Paul's explanation of the first words, the 'image of the invisible God'.

Notice also that the word firstborn is connected with being 'over all creation'. This is another meaning of firstborn, signifying dominion over all things as the firstborn member of the family was heir and lord of all, the one with supreme authority. Christ's authority is not something given to him by a higher authority, but rather it is absolute. Paul is never suggesting that Christ is the first of all created beings, but rather that He is unique, being distinguished from all creation, because, as he tells us in verse 16, He is the creator Himself.

28

(16) For by him all things were created: things in heaven and on earth, visible and invisible, whether thrones or powers or rulers or authorities; all things were created by him and for him.

This verse echoes the language of Genesis 1 and the OT Wisdom literature of Proverbs 8:22, 30. Christ is the craftsmen at the right hand of the Father, the physical manifestation of God creating all that has ever been created. John draws upon the Logos language of Plato to make the same point in the opening words of his gospel.

'In the beginning was the Word *(Logos)*, and the Word was with God *(Theos)*, and the Word was God'.

This verse has been twisted in a diabolical way in the Jehovah's Witnesses' New World Translation (NWT) which reads, 'and the Word was 'a' God', inserting the indefinite article 'a' into a translation from English. There are two reasons why the NWT is absolutely impossible. Firstly, the Greek text reads 'and God was the Word', rather than, 'the Word was God'. Our English versions have changed the order to make it read easier, but the Greek is emphatic. Secondly, there is no indefinite article 'a' in the Greek language. The NWT is a deliberate mistranslation to deceive and confuse. John categorically states, as does Paul, that Jesus Christ is God the Creator.

The second part of Paul's claim in verse 16 is aimed at the heresy in Colossae. He writes that Christ created all things, both visible and invisible and then gives a list of beings in a descending order of authority. This list includes the arch angels, lesser angels, fallen angels and other spiritual entities. Here he is laying the foundation of Christ's supreme authority in order to rebuke those who have been teaching the Gnostic claim of angelic authority. Jesus Christ is not 'an' authority, rather, He is 'the' authority, the one to whom these others owe their very existence. Why then, would any of his readers choose to obey a lesser authority than the Creator Himself, the one who redeemed them, who rescued them from the dominion of darkness?

Paul also tells us that all things were created 'for' Him. The universe, our world and every creature, have all been created *for* Christ. These words proclaim the eternal plan of God to glorify Himself. The Jewish rabbis taught that the world was created for the

Messiah, however, they didn't recognize Him when He came into the world He had made. Everything that has happened from the dawn of creation has been a part of God's plan of salvation, a plan designed to bring 'many sons to glory' (Hebrews: 2:10), to and for the praise of His glory. The Messiah's coming into this world was not a secondary rescue plan after the grand design went wrong, rather, the Fall was foreseen and allowed, and always under the supreme authority of His control.

In verse 17 Paul completes His initial explanation of who Christ is. *'He is before all things and in him all things hold together'*.

Again Paul underlines Christ as Creator being 'before all things', but in his last phrase he draws his readers into the language of the philosophers. When you look at a piece of wood what do you see, a solid, liquid, static or moving object? We would say a solid, static object. However, if you could look closer, indeed at the very atoms that make up the wood, you would find that they are all moving; millions of protons, neutrons and electrons spinning around in fluid motion at the speed of light, controlled and sustained by He who is the 'Light of the world'. And so it is with everything. Metal looks solid, but with extreme heat it becomes a liquid. 'In Him all things hold together'.

Paul is telling us that every atom is held together by the absolute knowledge and power of Jesus Christ. He is the ground and foundation of all reality; He is, as Aquinas stated years later, the 'Unmoved Mover'. The verse we read from Hebrews says the same thing, that He is the one who 'sustains all things'. He commands every atom to function as it does. How did He turn water into wine; He simply rearranged the atoms; how did He walk on water, He rearranged the atoms, how does He heal the body, He rearranges the atoms. He is the Lord of creation, all creation obeys His will; every atom obeys His will. Without his sustaining power there is no life, no world, and no universe.

Every person, every creature, owes the very breath in their lungs to His sustaining power. Those who know and love Him should live their lives in holy gratitude and worship (Romans 12:1-2), and those who refuse to acknowledge Him (Romans 1: 18-23), even though in their secret thoughts they know He is there, such will experience His wrath for suppressing the truth manifested all around them.

This then is the first part of Paul's answer to the question 'who is Jesus Christ?' He is the exact representation of the God-head, the physical manifestation of the Triune God, the Eternal One. He is not some created being as the Jehovah's Witnesses and others claim, on the contrary, Genesis One could read, 'in beginning Christ created the heavens and the earth'; John's gospel could read, 'in the beginning was Christ, and Christ was with God and God was Christ', and Paul means exactly the same thing when he says 'He is the image of the invisible God, the firstborn over all creation'.

Study Five

Who is Jesus Christ? (Part Two)

Colossians 1: 18-20

(v18) And he is the head of the body, the church; he is the beginning and the firstborn from among the dead, so that in everything he might have the supremacy. (19)For God was pleased to have all his fullness dwell in him (20) and through him to reconcile to himself all things, whether things on earth or things in heaven, by making peace through his blood, shed on the cross.

In this study we will examine the humanity of Jesus as it relates to the letter to the Colossians. Space does not allow for us to dig deeply into the theological issues, therefore, we will concentrate on how Jesus' humanity relates to us in our everyday lives.

These three verses are speaking of how God has accomplished reconciliation with fallen humanity through the sacrifice of Jesus on the cross. The Word (logos) has 'become flesh and dwelt among us' (John 1:14). God the Son became the Son of God, lived as a man, was crucified and rose again. He is the beginning of the Church and its head, the head of a new resurrection people who are *in* Him. He is the firstborn 'from among the dead' a term meaning the first in a series who will follow Him.

How has this been achieved? Why was it necessary for God the Son to become the Son of God? The answers to these questions are deeply theological and deserve an entire book, but for the Church in Colossae the issue was very specific. For the Colossians, the problem was the heresy of Gnosticism which claimed that the entire material world was evil. Gnostics claimed that Jesus only 'appeared' (*doce*) to be a real human being, a heresy we call 'Docetism'. The Docetists claimed Jesus couldn't be a real physical man or He would be tainted with evil like the whole of creation.

32

Paul refutes this idea categorically in 2:9 where he states; *'For in Christ all the fullness of Deity lives in bodily form...'* Paul is emphasizing that God was in a real body, not merely appearing to be real. Take a look at 1st John 1:1-2 where the Apostle John is making a similar refutation to Docetism. John says we saw and touched Him, we know He was real. Christ Himself makes this clear in Hebrews 10:5 which reads, *'therefore, when Christ came into the world, he said: "Sacrifice and offering you did not desire, but a body you prepared for me".*

Why is this so important to us?

The simple answer to that question is this. If Jesus Christ wasn't exactly like us in His humanity, then He cannot be a substitute for us, He cannot die in our place and reconcile us to God. In Leviticus chapter 27 we can read about the strict laws concerning the lamb that could be sacrificed for sin. Some people would try to substitute an animal which was not fit for the sacrifice, probably because they didn't want to lose the best of their flock. They tried to cheat. Those animal sacrifices were a shadow of what was to come. God was pointing to the future substitute in Christ who would perfectly fulfil God's demand for justice and 'make peace through his blood on the cross'. If Jesus was not a perfect substitute, Satan would have been the first to stand up and shout 'you can't die for them because you're not really one of them'.

Only a real human being, one just like us, could take our place, for God must be perfectly just. Those who teach that Jesus somehow had an advantage fail to understand the enormity of what He accomplished in His humanity. Hebrews 2:14 and 17 tell us that:

'Since the children have flesh and blood, he too shared in their humanity so that by his death he might destroy him who holds the power of dead...', and in verse 17, *'for this reason he had to be made like his brothers in every way, in order that he might become a merciful and faithful high priest in service to God, and that he might make atonement for the sins of the people'.*

Scripture clearly states that Jesus was made like us *in every way*, that He was a real man. There is much more we could say from a theological perspective, but in this study I want to concentrate on how that fact is a comfort for us, not only in that He has secured our eternal life, but in that He understands the challenges, trials and suffering that so often beset every one of us. But firstly, let's take a brief look at His dedication to accomplishing the Father's will.

We often hear messages about the suffering of Christ on the cross, and we may come away from those sermons with the idea that Jesus' suffering was only for the last day or two of His life. The Scriptures contradict this presumption entirely. As we saw in the previous study, Jesus Christ has always existed. It was He who created this world when He was with the Father in the beginning of creation. He knew that He would be crucified before He even started creation. He looked into the future and saw Himself being whipped until His flesh was ripped off His body, He saw the priests and soldiers punching and kicking Him, He saw them spitting in His face and the people shouting 'crucify Him', He saw Himself carrying the cross out of Jerusalem, His blood dripping on the cobble stones, His body covered with a horse blanket. He saw them throw Him on the ground, and He saw the soldiers hammer nails through His hands and feet and the cross lifted up. He saw the agony on His face and the people staring in horror. He saw all of this, yet He went ahead and created this world.

It is one thing to see the future from the position of glory, and perhaps quite another to take on the weakness of human flesh and live it in time. There is no doubt that Jesus knew that He would be crucified, and perhaps it was on His mind almost every day of His life. Just take a few moments to look up the many times He warned His disciples that He must go up to Jerusalem where He would be put to death. Here is a list from just one of the gospels. Matthew 12:40, 17:9, 12, 22, 20:18, 28, 26:2.

Did Jesus ever feel fear and apprehension about what lay ahead of Him? He wouldn't be a normal person if He didn't. We also know that Jesus spent much time alone in prayer. What was He praying about? No doubt He had seen people crucified; the Romans often left the bodies of runaway slaves and dissidents hanging on crosses on the roadside as a warning. Hebrews 5:7 gives us a clue as to one of the foremost topics He prayed throughout His life.

'During the days of Jesus' life on earth, he offered up prayers and petitions with loud cries and tears to the one who could save him from death, and he was heard because of his reverent submission'.

Sobering words! You and I, and every sinner, are the reason that Jesus had such agony during His life, and as the time of His death drew near. Jesus' prayers were heard, but the answer was always the same, as was His willingness to obey.

As the time grew closer, Jesus had to draw on His courage and resolve. In Luke 9:51 there is a word which tells us about how dedicated Jesus was in His devotion to save us. It says 'Jesus set out for Jerusalem *resolutely'*. Some versions say He looked up to heaven and then *set His face* towards Jerusalem, determined to complete His mission. What it means is this: He saw what was ahead and, like any man, He was full of dread at the reality of being crucified. However, He knew that only through His death could we be saved, so He held onto His courage and, motivated by pure love, set His face towards His death, and walked towards Jerusalem with absolute determination. That's how much He loves us; that's how dedicated He is to saving us.

In the Garden of Gethsemane He returned to the Father three times, asking if there was another way other than the cross. Such was His dedication to save us that He always surrendered to the Father's will, even to the point of shedding blood (Hebrews 12:4).

Yet there is much more we can say about the humanity of our Lord. Scripture says He was *'tempted in every way, just as we are'*, yet never sinned (Hebrews: 4:15). That verse alone should give us comfort, and encourage us to tell Him of our own temptations. He is the 'sympathetic high priest' who understands, empathises and gives power and relief to those who trust Him.

Jesus also experienced rejection, not only from the spiritual leaders of Israel, but even from the people of His hometown, and His personal family. In Luke 4:16-30 we read about how He returned to Nazareth and spoke in the local synagogue where everyone knew Him. After claiming that He was the One prophesied about in Isaiah, the people *'drove Him out of town, and took Him to the brow of the hill on which the town was built, in order to throw Him down the cliff'*. Jesus walked away from them. On a visit to Nazareth I stood above that cliff. It brought the text alive and reminded me of the depth of

35

rejection He suffered. Isaiah 53: 3 tells us 'He was despised and rejected by men, a man of sorrows and familiar with suffering'.

But how did He feel when His own mother and brothers decided that He had lost His mind (Mark 3:21) and came to take Him home? We have a saying in English that 'blood is thicker than water', but that day Jesus taught us that ' the relationship of Spirit is greater than that of blood' for 'whoever does God's will is my brother and sister and mother' (Mark 3:34).

How did He feel when His own mother believed Him to have lost His mind, the woman who had been visited by an angel in her youth, had given birth to Him in a stable, seen the shepherds and kings come to worship, the teachers of the law amazed at Him when He was twelve, and watched Him turn water into wine? How much did that betrayal wrench His heart?

And what can we say about the spiritual war He endured. We would be foolish to think that His temptation in the desert, at the beginning of His ministry, was the only time Satan attacked Him. Luke tells us that 'the devil left Him until an opportune time' (4:13). Jesus' ministry was full of demonic confrontations, all of which He won, but I believe that the enemy was often there, whispering in His ear, desperately trying to get Him to resist the Father's will just once. And how would it feel to the one who had resisted evil all of His life to be accused of being in league with Satan, the Prince of Evil, a charge the Pharisees levelled against Him on several occasions?

Summary

Understanding Jesus' humanity should make us take pause. Those who imply that, as the Son of God He somehow had an advantage over us, defame Him in the extreme. Such a teaching comes from ignorance of how His Divinity and humanity acted in harmony to achieve perfect justice for us. One of the earliest of Christian hymns from Philippians 2:5-10 brings clarity, encouragement and a challenge.

(5) Your attitude should be the same as that of Christ Jesus: (6) Who, being in very nature God, did not consider equality with God something to be grasped, (7) but made himself nothing, taking the very nature of a servant, being made in human likeness. (8) And being

found in appearance as a man, he humbled himself and became obedient to death - even death on a cross. (9) Therefore God exalted him to the highest place and gave him a name that is above every name, (10) that at the name of Jesus every knee should bow, in heaven and on earth, and every tongue confess that Jesus Christ is Lord, to the glory of God the Father.'

Study Six

Reconciled

Colossians 1:21-23

21 Once you were alienated from God and were enemies in your minds because of your evil behavior. 22 But now he has reconciled you by Christ's physical body through death to present you holy in his sight, without blemish and free from accusation— 23 if you continue in your faith, established and firm, and do not move from the hope held out in the gospel. This is the gospel that you heard and that has been proclaimed to every creature under heaven, and of which I, Paul, have become a servant.

These verses have often been used to say that salvation is conditional, that it relies on our 'continuing in the faith' in the sense that our performance determines our eternal outcome. These words are so often misunderstood because they are taken out of their context within this letter. In order to understand this issue we need to determine what salvation means for Paul, and how salvation is being presented in contemporary evangelism. This topic is discussed in depth in the first chapter of my book *Running the Race*, but here we will try to give a brief answer.

Throughout the New Testament there are summary verses to explain salvation. The most well known would be John 3:16 which reads, *'whoever believes in him shall not perish but have eternal life'*. The words 'believe in Him' have been so diluted by many evangelists that they in no way reflect Jesus' teachings. In the original, the command is to 'cast your whole weight upon', meaning to surrender your life entirely into the control of Christ and the will of God. This theology is taught without compromise throughout the NT. When a person does this, there is a death to self, a death to the rebellious ego which requires a new birth, and results in a new creation. If there is no 'death' there will be no 'new birth'.

If we teach some diluted version of this, such as 'ask Jesus into your heart', rather than' give your life to Christ', our Churches will be full of unregenerate people who are trying to live the Christian life on their own strength. Understand that the Holy Spirit does not take up permanent residence in those who want to tack Jesus onto their own lifestyle, His role is to regenerate those who have 'died with Christ', been 'crucified with Christ', 'buried with Christ', etc., to use but a few expressions relating to the spiritual experience of new birth.

Christ's call is to take up our cross (Mark 8:34-35), a reference to 'death to self', death to our ego, and to be willing to lose mother, father, brother, sister, and be a disciple (Luke 14: 26), but this is seldom taught today. Being born again is not a matter of believing in a historical Jesus, but surrendering our will, our entire life into the control of the living Christ. Look at a few verses in just this letter we are studying.

2:6. 'So then, just as you received Christ as Lord'.

Do we teach this today, or something like 'accept Jesus as your Saviour', as if Jesus Christ, the Creator of the world needed *our* acceptance? There is an eternal difference here. Lord means master, the one in control, the one we belong to, but some teach that we can 'accept' Jesus, as if He needed to be accepted by us. If Jesus Christ is not Lord of our life, He is not Saviour either; these two can never be separated. If we have never given our life to Christ then it still belongs to us, we are not 'God's own possession' (Eph 1:14).

2:20 'Since you died with Christ to the basic principles of this world...'.
3:3-4 'For you died, and your life is now hidden with Christ in God. When Christ, who is your life, appears, then you also will appear with him in glory'.

Those who teach that a Christian can walk away and reject Christ, therefore losing their salvation, have no idea what it means to have 'died with Christ'. These words of Paul are not just Christian rhetoric, but expressing a spiritual experience which is irreversible and absolute. Paul mentions the basic principles of this world. The principle he is speaking of is the root of all sin, wilful rebellion against God, refusal to submit to Christ as Lord, that which John clearly teaches in 1st John 3: 4-9.

Paul also says our lives are 'hidden with Christ in God' and that Christ '*is* our life'. For the born again person the old, egotistical, rebellious life is dead and a new creation has been resurrected. Those who have experienced this new birth can never 'walk away' because there is no old person to do the walking, that person died. Sadly, Churches are full of people who have never died with Christ, who continue to live their lives in the same way they did before they 'believed'.

I am sometimes asked if there is a simple test to know if we are truly born of God or not. My answer is this: 'If you belong to Jesus Christ, if you are God's possession; then you will always say 'yes Lord' when He commands you'. If you can easily say 'no Lord', then you should doubt that you belong to Him, or ever have. The true Christian always repents when his/her earthly nature (Colossians 3:5) rears its ugly head, but the counterfeit Christian has the idea that 'believer' and 'disciple' are two different levels of Christian. They want to be a believer, but not a disciple. Let's go back to chapter 1: 21-23 and see them in this context. Pauls says,

'if you continue in your faith, established and firm, not moved from the hope held out in the gospel'.

I said earlier that these words are both warning and promise. They are a warning to those who never become 'established and firm'. 'Established' is the initial experience of new birth, and 'firm' relates to the ongoing process of sanctification, which is the proof of a changed life. Such people can 'never be moved', because they are 'rooted and built up in Him' (2:6). Paul uses the word 'if' to challenge us to examine our lives honestly and see whether or not we were firstly established, and secondly, put down strong roots and became firm.

Jesus' well known parable of the sower in Matthew 13 has a very similar meaning. In this parable Jesus gives us the explanation of His teaching. The first group received the message of the kingdom but did not understand it. Like many today who hear a gospel that just tells them to say a sinners prayer, without explaining all that it means to be a disciple, these ones did not understand enough to make an informed decision to give their lives in surrender to God's will. Jesus tells us that Satan comes and snatches away what was sown in their hearts.

The second group also never took the time to count the cost. Jesus says that when troubles and persecution came along, because of the truth, these ones quickly fell away. This reminds me of those who preach that Jesus wants to give you a happy and abundant life, to give you 'your best life now' to quote one such teacher. Christ never promised such a thing, rather, He told us that we would be hated, persecuted and despised because of Him.

The third group are choked by the 'worries of the world and the deceitfulness of wealth'. Today, in many churches we hear what is loosely defined as the Prosperity Gospel, a counterfeit of the truth. Christ said we cannot serve two masters, God and money; we will love one and hate the other. When a person tries to do both their shallow faith is destroyed. Again, they never took root, were never established and firm.

But the last group Jesus mentions in Matthew 13:23 are different. He tells us that they heard the word and understood it. This is the only group who are said to have 'understood' the message. The message is to receive Christ as Lord, with all that implies about discipleship. If that is understood, and the person surrenders their life to Christ, they will experience new birth, death to self, taking up their cross and will be established in Him. These ones become 'rooted and grounded' in Him, to quote Ephesians, and will be 'firm'. Such a person, who has put down deep roots, cannot be moved from the hope held out in the gospel. Paul's use of the word 'if' was never saying that salvation is conditional upon our performance, rather, it is a challenge to examine if we have been established and become firm.

Therefore, these words are a promise to those who have been reconciled, those who trust absolutely and solely on Christ, the one they have 'received as Lord'. Paul says, in the previous verses, that these ones have been reconciled, that once they were 'alienated' and 'enemies of God in their minds', but now have been made 'holy in his sight, without blemish and free from accusation'. Such beautiful promises for those who have surrendered all into the Lord's care.

And finally, we must also understand that perseverance is one of the fruits of the Spirit, a fruit which is produced through trials, testings and suffering (James 1:3). Perseverance is the outworking of becoming firm. A young tree is often supported by a wooden stake to help it stand against the storms until it puts down deep roots and becomes firm. So it is with us, however, if we cast our whole weight upon Christ, as John 3:16 commands, then *He* is our foundation, and the storms of life will not move us.

Those who continue in their faith do so because the Holy Spirit produces His fruits in them, and these will endure to the end as the old gospel song states; 'we shall not, we shall not be moved'.

Study Seven

Mystery: Part One

Colossians 1:24-29

24 Now I rejoice in what I am suffering for you, and I fill up in my flesh what is still lacking in regard to Christ's afflictions, for the sake of his body, which is the church. 25 I have become its servant by the commission God gave me to present to you the word of God in its fullness— 26 the mystery that has been kept hidden for ages and generations, but is now disclosed to the Lord's people. 27 To them God has chosen to make known among the Gentiles the glorious riches of this mystery, which is Christ in you, the hope of glory. 28 He is the one we proclaim, admonishing and teaching everyone with all wisdom, so that we may present everyone fully mature in Christ. 29 To this end I strenuously contend with all the energy Christ so powerfully works in me.

In this section Paul speaks about two mysteries. In this study we will examine the first, which is in regard to his personal sufferings as an apostle and how these sufferings relate to Christ. Why do I consider this a mystery? I use this term because a mystery is something we cannot fully explain, even though we see the reality. Suffering in the service of Christ is such a mystery. As we shall see, Scripture clearly states that suffering is an integral part of the Christian's life, but what Divine purpose does it serve, and do those who choose to serve in the declaration of the gospel suffer more than those who are silent about their relationship with Christ? Ist Peter 1: 6-7 speaks about the trials and testing that all Christians must suffer.

6 In all this you greatly rejoice, though now for a little while you may have had to suffer grief in all kinds of trials. 7 These have come so that the proven genuineness of your faith—of greater worth than gold, which perishes even though refined by fire—may result in praise, glory and honour when Jesus Christ is revealed.

There is no apparent mystery here. Peter tells us why these trials come to us, namely, in order to prove that our faith in Christ is genuine. It is easy to praise God when all is going well, but what about when someone close to us is declared terminally ill, or we have great physical suffering, or lose someone close to us. In these moments our faith is tested. Will we succumb to the temptation and whisperings of the enemy, those angry thoughts which encourage us to say that God does not exist, or, that if He does, then He has no love for us, that He doesn't protect His own? There is no doubt in my mind that Satan uses these times to try and turn us against God.

The story of Job is very revealing in this context, for it not only reveals the test which proves the genuineness of faith, but also God's part and pleasure in the outcome of the test. Job had all that any person could want in the material world, and more. He had the deepest respect of the people around him; indeed, he was in a position of authority. Satan accused God of 'putting a hedge around Job', and had the audacity to tell God that Job would surely curse Him to His face if the Lord allowed him to take away His gifts. God allowed Satan to destroy Job's ungodly children, and to basically take all of his possessions. The man's wife also condemned him saying 'curse God and die'. But Job, although wretched and broken, refused to curse the Lord. He proved that his faith was genuine. But there is another side to this.

Do we stop and think about God's reaction in all of this? We can be so busy asking questions about *why* He has allowed our suffering that we fail to see something incredibly important to Him. I believe that it gives God great pleasure when His children continue to hold His hand and trust Him through the everyday storms of life. In fact, I believe He even steers us towards those storms in order to test and prove our faith, giving Him 'bragging rights' on our account. Consider the fact that it was the Lord Himself who pointed to Job in saying;

'Have you considered my servant Job? There is no one on earth like him; he is blameless and upright, a man who fears God and shuns evil'. (Job 1:8)

For me, and I may be mistaken, the Lord is very proud of Job, He takes delight in this man. Job's godliness gave the Lord pleasure, but more so, I believe that Job's faithfulness through the terrible trial he had brought great joy to God's heart. And so it is with us. Our trials and sufferings not only prove that we are truly God's children, but when we come through them trusting Him, even though buffered and attacked by Satan, I believe the Lord rejoices in His decision to adopt us as His children. Consider the story of Jesus taking the disciples across the Sea of Galilee (often called a lake) and into a storm, from Luke 8: 22-15.

22 One day Jesus said to his disciples, "Let us go over to the other side of the lake." So they got into a boat and set out. 23 As they sailed, he fell asleep. A squall came down on the lake, so that the boat was being swamped, and they were in great danger. 24 The disciples went and woke him, saying, "Master, Master, we're going to drown!" He got up and rebuked the wind and the raging waters; the storm subsided, and all was calm. 25 "Where is your faith?" he asked his disciples. In fear and amazement they asked one another, "Who is this? He commands even the winds and the water, and they obey him."

Several of Jesus' disciples were experienced fishermen and knew this sea well. Such men knew the weather patterns and would most likely know if there was a good chance of a dangerous storm getting up. Apart from that, Jesus knew the future; He knew without doubt that a storm would come, and He purposely set out to cross the lake. He gets into the boat and goes to sleep. The storm comes and is so violent it's swamping the boat, but Jesus just keeps on sleeping, looking to all intents and purposes as though He is unaware that they are all about to drown. The disciples wake Him up, probably, in their minds, to give Him the chance to throw off His robe and swim for His life. But Jesus gets up, rebukes the storm and asks them 'where is your faith'?

I love this story and imagine that Jesus may have been lying there with His eyes closed listening to them getting more and more anxious, just waiting for one of them to say 'don't worry guys, Jesus is with us'. It's pretty difficult to sleep when a boat is being 'swamped' with water. But none of them had the faith to trust they would be safe while He was with them. By this time they had all seen Him turn water to wine, heal a man with leprosy, a paralytic, the centurion's servant, raise a widow's son from the dead, etc., but they still had no real, genuine faith. In essence, they failed the test.

God will lead into storms, but He is there in the boat. I strongly suspect that if any one of them had said 'we have nothing to fear while He is with us', that the test would have been passed and the storm may have simply abated. But what of this mystery I alluded to earlier? Paul writes to the Colossians in verse 24 of our text;

'I rejoice in what I am suffering for you, and I fill up in my flesh what is still lacking in regard to Christ's afflictions, for the sake of his body, which is the church'.

What does he mean when he writes; 'what is still lacking in regard to Christ's afflictions'? Surely he is not speaking of the Lord's suffering on the cross. No! That is finished, 'it is accomplished' as the Lord Himself said. Rather, Paul is speaking of the 'Body of Christ', the Church which must suffer between His first coming into the world to die for sins, and His second coming to judge sin. Galatians 4:4 tells us that 'in the fullness of time', Christ came into this world, the perfect time, and He will return at the perfect time. Until that time we, His body, are filling up in our flesh what is still lacking, still to complete.

We are the Body of Christ, and as we suffer, He suffers. No one can be saved but through the suffering of Christ. In order for Him to win our souls and give us eternal life, He suffered. But is there also a sense that if we are to be partners with Him in soul-winning, that we too must be willing to suffer? I believe that there is, and this is the mystery I wish to bring our attention to. It is one thing to have personal tests and trials which prove our faith, and still another to suffer in the service of Christ as the Body of Christ. The first form of suffering refers to proving our salvation is genuine, but the second has to do with our reward for serving Him in His will and by His power. Paul understood this principle when he wrote to the Philippians in chapter 1:27-30.

[27] Whatever happens, conduct yourselves in a manner worthy of the gospel of Christ. Then, whether I come and see you or only hear about you in my absence, I will know that you stand firm in the one Spirit, striving together as one for the faith of the gospel [28] without being frightened in any way by those who oppose you. This is a sign to

them that they will be destroyed, but that you will be saved—and that by God. [29] For it has been granted to you on behalf of Christ not only to believe in him, but also to suffer for him, [30] since you are going through the same struggle you saw I had, and now hear that I still have.

There is an underlying message here for those who 'strive together as one for the faith of the gospel'. They will be opposed, not only by men, but also under the spiritual attack Paul wrote of in Ephesians 6: 10-20. In verse 19 of that passage Paul asks,

'pray also for me, that whenever I open my mouth, words may be given me so that I will fearlessly make known the mystery of the gospel, for which I am an ambassador in chains'.

The parable of the talents (Matthew 25: 14-30) has a similar message. Each person was given certain talents of money, which correspond to the gifts and talents each receives at birth, and also at new birth. Some used them wisely, and others unwisely, but the one who strove to make an increase received the greatest reward. The man who hid his talents was never born again; his attitude was that the master was a 'hard man'; he didn't personally know the heart of Christ at all.

Every Christian can decide what to do with what he/she has been given. When your Church is planning a local evangelistic event, or short-term mission to a third world country and needs cooks, builders, teachers, etc., at these times we make decisions about how we 'invest' our talents. If we choose to make ourselves vulnerable and go, we may well suffer hardships we could have avoided, but if we choose to stay at home within our comfort zones, we may not only miss out on the life-changing experience of being involved in soul-winning, but also forfeit the reward the Lord had planned for us.

Paul understood that suffering was an integral part of his ministry as an apostle. God allowed this man to be tested by Satan in terribly frightening and painful circumstances. He spent a night in the open sea, was shipwrecked, almost stoned to death on several occasions, flogged and hunted. But Paul didn't indulge himself in self-pity trips, rather he 'pressed on toward the goal', understanding that he was part of this 'filling up the afflictions of Christ' in his own body, showing in his willingness to suffer that he lived for eternal values, not temporal ones. He rejoiced in the knowledge that he was imitating His Lord's suffering as part of the Body of Christ here on earth. He saw his chains as a triumph, not a punishment from God, but an honor, and he counted himself extremely fortunate to be given the opportunity to serve in this way. In Philippians 1: 12-14 he writes,

12 Now I want you to know, brothers and sisters, that what has happened to me has actually served to advance the gospel. 13 As a result, it has become clear throughout the whole palace guard and to everyone else that I am in chains for Christ. 14 And because of my chains, most of the brothers and sisters have become confident in the Lord and dare all the more to proclaim the gospel without fear.

In Summary

Like the disciples Jesus took with Him in the boat, we cannot see clearly what is ahead of us, or where the Lord is leading us. But it is His prerogative to test us, to prove our faith genuine, the faith which is of 'greater worth than gold' (1st Peter 1:7), the faith that gives Him pleasure. Our part is to hold His hand and let go of fear, self-pity and trust His Lordship.

And there are very few, if any, people who have seen the demonic forces which actively oppose those who work in partnership with the Lord to win souls. If we could, even the bravest of us might shrink away in fear. But Christ has conquered them, and He leads us in the spiritual battle to bring light into the dark places. Every Christian has a part to play in the Body of Christ, and our passion for the lost, if indeed we have one, will be tested. We may suffer, and in our suffering prove that, like the One who dwells within us, we are compelled by love to bring and shine the light that we have received.

Study Eight

Mystery: Part Two

Colossians 1:24-29

²⁴ Now I rejoice in what I am suffering for you, and I fill up in my flesh what is still lacking in regard to Christ's afflictions, for the sake of his body, which is the church. ²⁵ I have become its servant by the commission God gave me to present to you the word of God in its fullness— ²⁶ the mystery that has been kept hidden for ages and generations, but is now disclosed to the Lord's people. ²⁷ To them God has chosen to make known among the Gentiles the glorious riches of this mystery, which is Christ in you, the hope of glory. ²⁸ He is the one we proclaim, admonishing and teaching everyone with all wisdom, so that we may present everyone fully mature in Christ. ²⁹ To this end I strenuously contend with all the energy Christ so powerfully works in me.

The Church in Colossae was infiltrated by Gnostics. They were teaching that there were higher levels of spirituality and power for people to reach forms of perfection and ecstatic experiences. Early Church writers often refer to the father of this form of Gnosticism as Simon the Sorcerer, the man Peter encountered in Acts 8. Within a year of the Day of Pentecost the evangelist Philip set off to Samaria, probably soon after persecution broke out in Jerusalem immediately after Stephen was martyred. He preached a gospel of baptism into the name of Jesus Christ, but the Holy Spirit entered none of those who believed. Perhaps the reason for this was that the Lord wanted a unified Church and used Peter firstly to the Jews, then half-Jews (Samaritans) and finally Gentiles (Cornelius family).

Simon was a sorcerer; his interest was not in salvation, but power, and he delighted in people calling him the 'Great Power' (Acts 8:10). He thought that baptism would enhance his demonic power, but it didn't. When Peter and John arrived, Simon saw that the Holy Spirit entered these first Samaritan believers through the laying on of hands, however, The Holy Spirit never entered this man. He offered to buy this power, failing to understand the basic principle of death to one's ego. Simon's ego was well and truly alive. Peter told him he was *'full of bitterness and captive to sin'* (8:23), a far cry from a born again man.

That bitterness led Simon on a demonic path to destroy the Church from within. The early Church writers, such as Irenaeus in his *Against Heresies*, go into great detail about Simon's life and influence, as Gnosticism spread like a fire. Over 30 Gnostic gospels were written, all of which were rejected by early Church leaders, and many of them still survive today. This form of Gnosticism was in its infancy here in Colossae, a religion that loved the word 'mystery', like so many New Age religions today. Paul counters their teachings by pointing to the greatest mystery of all, one that had been hidden for ages and generations, the mystery of new birth, the mystery of Christ in us.

I wonder how often we actually stop and meditate on the incredible privilege we have been given, the privilege of having, knowing and experiencing Christ dwelling in us. In the book of Hebrews, chapter 11, we can read about the Old Testament saints who never experienced what some Christians may even take for granted. These people had faith, yet at best only experienced the Spirit of God *upon* them for brief periods of their lives; none of them knew the privilege of *Christ in us, the hope of glory.* Do you remember our battle with sin before Christ came to live in us, how hopelessly enslaved we were to the demands of our fleshly desires? Could we have stood in faith as the saints of old did? Hebrews 11: 35-38 tells us that some of them:

···*were tortured, refusing to be released so that they might gain an even better resurrection. *[36]* Some faced jeers and flogging, and even chains and imprisonment. *[37]* They were put to death by stoning; they were sawed in two; they were killed by the sword. They went about in sheepskins and goatskins, destitute, persecuted and mistreated —* *[38]* the world was not worthy of them. They wandered in deserts and mountains, living in caves and in holes in the ground.*

And then the writer to Hebrews tells us the reason for mentioning them, his message to us.

³⁹ These were all commended for their faith, yet none of them received what had been promised, ⁴⁰ since God had planned something better for us so that only together with us would they be made perfect.

This was the mystery kept hidden for ages and generations; that we might be made perfect through the blood of Christ, sealed in Him through the indwelling Spirit, and empowered to live for Him. God had planned something better for us, a new covenant. Hebrews 10: 5-7 records the words of Christ regarding these things:

⁵ Therefore, when Christ came into the world, he said: "Sacrifice and offering you did not desire, but a body you prepared for me; ⁶ with burnt offerings and sin offerings you were not pleased. ⁷ Then I said, 'Here I am—it is written about me in the scroll— I have come to do your will, my God.'"

In verse 14 of the same chapter we read a beautiful, brief summary of what the mystery of Christ in us has achieved;

'Because by one sacrifice he has made perfect forever those who are being made holy'.

This precious gift Paul calls the 'glorious riches of this mystery', and we do well to meditate on God's gift every day, lest we become ungrateful children. Paul's message to the Colossians is the same message to us. It is in Christ that we are made perfect, in Him *'are hidden all the treasures of wisdom and knowledge'*. In other words, He is all we need, for He is everything. Without His indwelling presence we would have no power over the sin that previously enslaved us.

Jesus' disciples failed to understand this message, even after walking with Him for three years. In John 14 Jesus comforted them, knowing beforehand what would happen when they faced arrest. He knew they would flee in fear. He told them of the Holy Spirit who was *'with* them and would be *in* them' (17), that He would *'not leave them as orphans'* but come to them personally (18) and then said;

'on that day you will realize that I am in my Father, and you are in me, and I am in you' (20).

On the night Jesus was arrested they all ran. Peter denied Him three times, the One he swore he would die for. But on the day that Jesus' had promised, the Day of Pentecost, God's plan and promise were fulfilled, and for the first time human beings were filled with the Holy Spirit. Christ came to dwell in us, to make His home in us. Peter was changed instantly, and fearlessly proclaimed the gospel for the rest of his life until, as tradition claims, he was crucified in the Circus Maximus in Rome before a huge crowd, while Simon the Sorcerer watched on. Simon, the one that Peter had warned was 'full of bitterness and captive to sin' in Acts chapter 8, had become a personal friend of the Emperor Nero, impressing the ruler with his satanic ability to levitate. My novel, *Simon and Simon: Passion and Power* tells this story.

There are some important warnings in Colossians for Christians today, especially to those who are tempted to live their lives from one ecstatic experience to another. From the perspective of one who was saved out of satanic forms of the New Age Movement, I am deeply concerned when I see elements of esoteric and Eastern religious teachings creeping into the Church. I seriously doubt that those who seek such experiences have ever known the mystery of Christ in us. Many liberals, and others, advertise yoga, visualization, martial arts, etc., in their Church notices, and all of these have roots in demonic worship, but the most dangerous trend I believe comes in the guise of a counterfeit version of the Holy Spirit.

The Holy Spirit is the third 'persona' of the Triune God. He is not an 'it', an energy that can be used to 'slay people in the spirit', or to give them pseudo drunken weekends such as 'Sloshfest' claims, when young adults meet to receive some 'anointing' and become 'drunk in the spirit'. Nor does He make people shake uncontrollably, utter gibberish while thrashing about on the floor, or crawl about on their hands and knees making animal noises. I have witnessed all of the above in so-called Churches, but none of these phenomena were new to me, for New Age practitioners experience such things on a daily basis. Let me state categorically that I believe they are demonic and not the work of the Holy Spirit of God!

In John 16 Jesus explains the work of the Holy Spirit. Jesus message is that the Spirit will guide us into truth, that He will not seek glory for Himself, but always point us to Christ. It is only in the past several decades that people have practiced worshipping the Holy Spirit and placing Him in the center rather than Christ. He will never be in that place, but if people insist on having continual ecstatic spiritual experiences, rather than level-headed Christian maturity, Satan is only too happy to provide them with a counterfeit which they presume and insist is the Spirit of God. In Colossians 2: 9-10 Paul tells us:

'For in Christ all the fullness of Deity lives in bodily form, and you have been given fullness in Christ, who is the head over every power and authority'.

The Scriptures declare that we have been given fullness in Christ, but, like spoiled children, so many professing Christians are running around shouting 'give me more, give me more'. They are not crying out for maturity, for maturity comes through suffering, trials and perseverance in hardships, rather, they are crying out for more ecstatic experiences. I believe that such 'faith' is either incredibly disillusioned or shallow, or has simply bypassed the true gospel which demands that we 'take up our cross'. It is 'another gospel', not the gospel of Christ. He promised that the world would hate us, that it would persecute us, but some Churches want to welcome the world and its master, the 'god of this world' (2nd Corinthians 4:4) in the door to entertain and make them feel good.

Such is the spirit of Gnosticism which was in Colossae and has resurrected in these Last Days. We must not allow such a spirit to deceive us, for we are the people of the new covenant, the people who can and do experience 'the mystery of Christ in us', the hope of glory.

Study Nine

Christ: Our Treasure

Colossians 1: 28 - 2:10

28 We proclaim him, admonishing and teaching everyone with all wisdom, so that we may present everyone perfect in Christ. 29 To this end I labor, struggling with all his energy, which so powerfully works in me.

2 I want you to know how much I am struggling for you and for those at Laodicea, and for all who have not met me personally. 2 My purpose is that they may be encouraged in heart and united in love, so that they may have the full riches of complete understanding, in order that they may know the mystery of God, namely Christ, 3 in whom are hidden all the treasures of wisdom and knowledge. 4 I tell you this so that no one may deceive you by fine-sounding arguments. 5 For though I am absent from you in body, I am present with you in spirit and delight to see how orderly you are and how firm your faith in Christ is.

In this study I want to ask two questions. What kind of pastor leads the congregation you attend, and what do you consider to be your treasure? In study seven we examined Paul's statement about his suffering for the sake of the gospel and the myriad physical trials he went through. In the first verses of this passage he again speaks about his struggles and labor. There is a great lesson and challenge here for those who claim the title of pastor, minister and even home-group leader. In Protestant Churches today, especially amongst Charismatics and Pentecostals, claiming labels has become very popular. But I truly wonder if those who desire to be called such titles have any real idea of the responsibility that comes *with* the title.

Paul says that he 'labors' (kopiao), 'struggling' (agonizomai) with all His energy. These two words underline the attitude of Paul as a servant of God. Although he gives Christ the glory for the energy he receives to struggle, none-the-less it is the apostle himself who, in his passion to 'present everyone perfect in Christ', works tirelessly, contending as a boxer training and fighting for a prize. These words convey the impression of contending against an enemy to the point of exhaustion. Paul had never met most of those at Colossae face to face, yet he considered them his responsibility, as Epaphras had shared the gospel on behalf of the apostle (1:7).

Paul was a true shepherd, a true soul-carer. Unlike so many self-proclaimed leaders today, he was not promoting himself in order to receive accolades, but rather fighting on his knees for those in his charge. He knew that wolves had come in among the flock in Colossae and Laodicea, and he could not be there in body to confront them. Like a parent knowing that their child is in danger, Paul contends for his children. Too many Christians today want the title without the responsibility, and therein lies the challenge. Do we as leaders contend on our knees for those we claim to be shepherds over? So often I see Christians calling themselves pastor this or apostle that on social media sites, but in reality these folk are all about self-promotion rather than true leadership.

The true leader is a servant, one who undergirds, admonishes, teaches and fights for the souls in his care, on behalf of Jesus Christ, and in His power.

Paul's purpose; *'to present everyone perfect in Christ'*. Hebrews 10:14 tells us that by one sacrifice, Christ 'has made perfect forever those who are being made holy'. Was Paul suggesting that he could make his charges perfect? Absolutely not! Only Jesus Christ can give us a declaration of perfection, and only He, through the transforming work of the Holy Spirit, can make us holy. The picture Paul paints here is of the striving pastor who contends with the enemy, interceding for his flock, teaching and admonishing them in order to present them to Christ. Like a proud father on his daughter's wedding day, Paul depicts himself as presenting us to our bridegroom, spotless, holy and beautiful.

Paul also states that he teaches 'with all wisdom'. What we teach is of vital importance. Paul mentions the Church at Laodicea, and in Revelation 3 we read the Lord's words regarding this Church which claimed *'I am rich; I have acquired wealth and do not need a thing'*. This was the lukewarm congregation that was about to be spewed out of the mouth of God, the Church which Christ counselled to *'buy gold refined in the fire'*. The Laodicean Church was suffering from an early Church dose of 'Prosperity Doctrine'. They were nominal, rich Christians who rebuked any kind of suffering for Christ, the trials and tests that 'prove our faith genuine' (1st Peter 1: 6-7).

What was being taught to these people? We don't know for certain, but whatever it was, it was not the wisdom of God's Word, but a counterfeit gospel which produced counterfeit Christians, and I suspect, a doctrine similar to that which is being preached in many 1st World countries today. What an insult to Christ to preach that God wants to give us 'our best life now', that the gospel is all about material abundance, perfect physical health and a life free of trials and testings.

In all of His earthly ministry, Jesus has not one positive word to say about material wealth, and a good deal of warnings about the dangers of money. Paul warned that the love of money could lead into all kinds of evils, and the Church at Laodicea had fallen in-love with money and out of love with Christ. Paul says in 2:1 of our text that he was struggling for this Church, fighting on his knees that they would return to sound, biblical wisdom. He goes on to tell them that his purpose is that

'they may be encouraged in heart and united in love, so that they may have the riches of complete understanding, in order that they may know the mystery of God, namely Christ, in whom are hidden all the treasures of wisdom and knowledge'.

To the Laodiceans, and those who hold to doctrines of prosperity, Paul says to seek the riches of full understanding which are found in all the treasures of Christ. Christ is 'the treasure hidden in the field' and the 'pearl of great price' (Matt 13:44-46), the treasure which requires that we give everything in order to attain Him. He is not a six figure bank account, a private jet or limousine, He is that Eternal Life, the one who is preparing a place in His Father's mansion, the one in whom all the riches of the world are nothing but impoverishment in comparison. If money is still our master, we must sincerely ask ourselves if Christ is Lord at all. He said we would love one and hate the other, that we cannot have two masters, so let us be sure that what we are listening to from the pulpit and stage is real wisdom, and not that which simply tickles itching ears.

To the Colossians Paul's message is *'that in Christ are hidden all the treasures of wisdom and knowledge'*. The word 'hidden' that he used does not mean something which is concealed, but rather stored-up. There is no knowledge outside of Christ which can save or 'present us perfect before Him'. As we have previously discovered, certain men in Colossae were teaching Gnostic ideas about mysteries and secret knowledge which was disclosed only to the elite. Much of that false teaching was closely tied to forms of Eastern mysticism, and like the prosperity theology of the Laodiceans, has found its way into the contemporary Church in various forms today.

To both Churches, Paul's desire is that *'they may know the mystery of God, namely Christ...'*. Those who teach counterfeit gospels produce counterfeit Christians, and it is my conviction that we have Churches today in which many such people attend week after week. Do these people 'know the mystery of God who is Christ Jesus', or some other Jesus they have invented, an idol which speaks through the mouth of a false teacher, telling them what they want to hear? Are these people so devoid of Christ that they need Eastern mysticism and material wealth to try and fill up what they lack in Christ? If we do not know Jesus Christ, He who is the mystery of God, if we do not know the 'hope of glory' which is 'Christ in us', then that emptiness which cries out in every unregenerate soul will try to be filled with whatever is offered.

Paul also tells them that his purpose is that

'they be encouraged in heart and united in love, so that they may have the full riches of complete understanding...'

Paul understands the dangers which are present in Colossae, but instead of rebuke he points to Christ. The old hymn tells us to *'turn our eyes upon Jesus, look full in his wonderful face, then the things of earth will grow strangely dim'*. This is always the key to complete understanding and unity within the Church. The false teachers were threatening that unity by advocating different levels of spirituality, a sure way of bringing envy, jealousy and egoism into their midst. When we take our eyes off Christ and start to compare ourselves with others, we immediately start using the principles of the world and forfeit the principles of humble service in Christ.

Paul says that he tells them these things

'so that no one may deceive them with fine-sounding arguments'.

The wolf in sheep's clothing knows how to dilute and pervert the Word of God, and how to add his own ingredients to make it palatable to people starving for truth. Christ will deal with these self-titled leaders in His own time, but still hold their listeners responsible for not searching the Scriptures to discern the truth.

In Summary

The passage we are studying begins with the words 'we proclaim Him'. In other letters Paul tells us that he 'preaches Christ crucified'. Is the Church you attend doing the same? The lesson of this study is that if we dare to look outside of Jesus Christ for our satisfaction, purpose and fulfilment in life, we will be bitterly disappointed and vulnerable to deception. There is no person alive who has plumbed the depths of wisdom and discovered the fullness of the treasure that is Jesus Christ; that is something which will take an eternity, yet this must be our goal.

And there is a challenge to each of us who claim to know Him. Are we practicing the compromise Christianity of the Laodiceans and allowing greedy men to lead us down a road of lukewarm faith which makes the Lord want to vomit? In the country where I serve, Ukraine, few churches that preach prosperity theology survive. Yes, they may start with a hiss and a roar, promising abundance and prosperity to their members, but eventually, many people begin to look closer and see that the majority are making a tiny minority wealthy. Just recently I had four people arrive at my mid-week Bible Study from Moscow. I'd never met them before, and discovered that all had been attending a Charismatic Church in that Russian city which was established by a millionaire 'pastor' from America. All of them had also completed a 3 year course in this church's seminary.

At one stage during our study one of the men started making claims about God's desire to make us wealthy, to never have sicknesses, etc., quoting some Old Testament verses out of context.

He spoke about the founder of their church and seminary and the teachings they adhered to. I let him speak for about ten minutes until one of my regular student-aged attendants asked me to comment. I asked all of these people how long they had attended this church, and the answer was 'four years'. I asked them if during that time the Lord had made them prosperous and completely healthy and, instead of preaching this doctrine, to show the fruit of it.

In truth, they had had to borrow money to attend the seminary and were desperately looking for jobs or sponsors to repay their loans. None of them owned a car and two had failing health. I asked them if their pastor, a man I knew of, was still flying back and forth in his private jet and going to church in his expensive European car with his body-guard escort. I asked them why, if they were so adamant about this theology being the truth, that God had not fulfilled what they understood as His promises in their own lives? They had no answers to these fundamental questions. I then asked them to please show us a single verse in the New Testament which suggested that Christians were to be materially rich and perpetually healthy. Again they were silent. My questions were put politely and sincerely, yet they took great offence and decided to leave, although two of them stayed and had a simple meal and prayer with us.

The truth of Scripture is simple: Jesus Christ is our treasure, an immeasurable and eternal treasure, for we who are sojourners on this earth, aliens, and ambassadors of His Kingdom. If we have been born of God, then we are no longer of this world, just passing through, and our inheritance is in Him. If we truly believe that, and trust Him to supply all our needs, then why do so many continue to live like citizens of the world? If we gave our lives to Christ, we belong to Christ. If we claim He is Lord, are we willing for Him to make us vulnerable, willing to allow Him to test our faith? These are serious questions which we will continue to examine as we move further into this letter to the Colossians.

Study Ten

Christic as Lord

Colossians 2: 6-7

6 *So then, just as you received Christ as Lord, continue to live in him,* 7 *rooted and built up in him, strengthened in the faith as you were taught, and overflowing with thankfulness.*

Imagine you are living in the late 1st century, or in a 21st century country where Christianity is banned or violently persecuted. You belong to a small Church community who support one another, and the Lord is adding new converts to His Church on a weekly basis. If you had the opportunity to witness to someone in that environment, what would you tell them if they asked you what it meant to *'receive Christ as Lord'*? There is an old saying from the early Church era; 'where there is persecution, there are few goats within the Church'.

For the first 300 years of Christian witness, there were few decades in which Christians were not at odds with the Roman Empire. Those years saw thousands murdered at the hands of the Romans, and yet the Church flourished to such an extent that by the time the Emperor Constantine decided to declare the empire 'Christian', in the early fourth century, it is estimated that between 12-15% were practicing Christians. In third world countries such as Iraq, Afghanistan, Pakistan, China and parts of Africa, there is still violent persecution against Christians, especially where Islamic law predominates.

Sadly, there is a marked contrast in the depth of Christian theology in many of these countries as well. Hyper-Pentecostal preachers of the 'word of faith' variety have drawn huge crowds in African countries where people seek healing and wealth, and it is estimated that over 80% of those who 'repent' at these meetings never actually go on in faith or produce fruit in accordance with regeneration. Others, such as those in China and Iran, where the threat of death comes with conversion, the Word of God and the cost of salvation is taken very seriously.

In 1st world countries we are experiencing a massive percentage of Churches replacing sound Biblical teachings with shallow experiential theology. In my opinion, the fault lies primarily in a lack of understanding of the fundamentals of salvation. For a detailed discussion on this topic see chapter one of my book *Running the Race*, but here we will outline the main points.

When the Apostle Peter preached his first sermon to Jews in Jerusalem, 3000 repented and received Christ as Lord. If we take this event out of context, and apply it to say modern American or British culture, we may well make the mistake of thinking that a person who is basically ignorant of the Bible's story of salvation can be born again after one simple sermon. God spent over 1300 years educating the Jews about the coming of Christ. These people understood the need of sacrifice, the idea of atonement, the Law of God, and that salvation required an unconditional surrender to the will of God. Is that what we preach today, or do we rather try and make our services cool, exciting and seeker friendly, or present Christ as some sort of Father Christmas figure who has a big bag of presents for those who will tolerate Him in their busy lives? When I ask 1st world Christians what is required for salvation I'm often quoted Scriptures such as the following. Romans 10: 9-10;

'That if you confess with your mouth "Jesus is Lord," and believe in your heart that God raised him from the dead, you will be saved. For it is with your heart that you believe and are justified, and it is with your mouth that you confess and are saved'.

It sounds simple enough, however, does the person they are quoting these verses to understand the words, 'confess, believe, justified and salvation'? The answer is usually that it isn't necessary for a seeker to understand these things at the beginning. I beg to differ, and so does my Bible. Imagine, instead of quoting Romans 10, we used other passages such as the following;

Luke 14:26-27. *If anyone comes to me and does not hate his father and mother, his wife and children, his brothers and sisters -*

yes, even his own life - he cannot be my disciple. And anyone who does not carry his cross cannot be my disciple.

Matthew 7:21. *Not everyone who says to me "Lord, Lord," will enter the kingdom of heaven, but only he who does the will of my Father who is in heaven."*

Jesus never told people to 'ask Him into their heart', rather, He used many metaphors associated with death to self, and parables which explained that only giving everything, the complete surrender of our wills to the will of God, would result in being 'born again'. In our evangelical meetings, do we stress the vile nature of sin; do we present Christ as Lord, or offer a form of cheap grace with the idea that people can have Jesus as a Savior now, and work on having Him as Lord later? And do we think that a person, who is virtually ignorant of the requirements of salvation, can simply say a 'sinner's prayer' and the Holy Spirit will be obliged to regenerate and fill them?

In a previous study we mentioned Simon the Sorcerer of Acts 8. This man 'repented and was baptized', yet he never received the Holy Spirit for he was still 'full of bitterness and a captive to sin'. God will not take up residence in any human soul until He decides that person is ready to die to self, for only after a death to our self will, and surrender to God's will, will we have the necessity of new birth. Without death to self (Romans 6:6), without being 'crucified with Christ'(Galatians 2:20), there is no need for 'new birth'.

In our chosen passage Paul mentions a wonderful progression of those who have received Christ as Lord. These are the marks of real regeneration, without which we should question if regeneration has occurred at all.

1. 'continue to live in Him'.

Living 'in Christ' is the ongoing surrender to His will, the 'taking up of our cross *daily*' (Luke 9:23). Regeneration occurs when we initially surrender our lives to the will of God, coming to the cross with repentant hearts to be free from our slavery to sin, with open hands and in the knowledge that He, and only He, is Lord, Savior, Redeemer and Sanctifier. Sanctification and transformation occur when we practice this every day, a joyful surrender to the one who is making us like Him.

2. '...rooted and built up in Him'.

As previously mentioned, Jesus once told a parable about a man who sowed seeds (Matthew 13). Jesus is speaking of people who heard the word of God and their reaction to it. This is one of the few parables where Jesus gives us an interpretation of the parable. The first two groups received the word with joy, but persecution and love of the world meant that they never put down roots. These were both fruitless. They heard the very same message, repented, but were never born of God. When Jesus speaks of the third group He says that they 'understood the message'. His point is that they considered the cost of salvation, that persecution would come, that regeneration requires them to walk away from the world, and these ones 'received Him as Lord'. The seed has to die in order to be reborn, and so it is with true salvation.

The apostle uses two metaphors in Colossians 2:7. Being rooted in Christ, whereby we produce fruit in accordance with repentance, and built up, a metaphor for building on the foundation which is Christ. Jesus told the well-known parable of the two men who built on sand and a rock to illustrate the importance of Scriptural foundations, and so must we.

3. '...strengthened in the faith as you were taught'.

Faith is strengthened through the refining principle of testing and trials (1st Peter 1:7). This phrase of Paul's connects with His words 'continue in Him' and echoes the same phrase in 1:23 where He tells them to be 'not moved from the hope held out in the gospel'. The old gospel song claimed 'we shall not, we shall not be moved', a word of encouragement to stand firmly on the foundation that is Christ and to 'walk as Jesus walked', allowing Him to lead us where and when He wills. He may lead us beside still waters and also into the storm, but His purpose will always be to strengthen us in the faith to the praise of His glory, to present us faultless.

4. '...and overflowing with thankfulness'.

If we take our eyes of Christ and let them descend to the world, our cup of thankfulness, our offering to Him, will be like the dregs which settle on the bottom. Those who continue in Him, taking up their cross daily, keeping their eyes upon Christ, will overflow with thankfulness, the cup will not be able to contain the gratitude we have. Emptiness comes from seeking fulfilment in empty things; fulfilment comes from our continual submission to eternal things. Paul wrote that 'godliness with contentment is of great gain' (1st Timothy 6:6). He writes those words in a passage warning people of the snare of wealth, of believing the lie that riches can satisfy. The Christian who is grateful for what the Lord has provided is a Christian who will overflow with thankfulness, for such a person understands that Christ labors in His Father's house preparing a place for them, guarding their inheritance (1st Peter 1:4), and transforming them into His likeness.

Paul's warning to the Colossians and to us is simply this. Do not believe the lie that there is something else that can satisfy, that there is something or someone which can fulfil us outside of Jesus Christ. Everything that the Lord gives us is to draw us more closely into Him, the only source of real life. Satan will offer a myriad of nicely packaged counterfeits, but his intention is always to destroy, to tempt and to fill us with dissatisfaction towards our Lord. Satan was given the greatest gifts by his Creator. He was the one who was ' the model of perfection, full of beauty and wisdom' (Ezekiel 28:12), but instead of overflowing with thankfulness he allowed God's gifts to make him vain and rebellious. Be diligent, therefore, to hold God's gifts in open hands, lest we take our eyes off the giver and seek satisfaction in the gift.

In Summary

Those who want Jesus Christ as a Savior, while retaining the authority to live as they please, are like the seed which will never bear fruit. True repentance requires an opposite change in direction, away from the life of sin which enslaved us, and into a life walking with the One who can destroy the root of rebellion and plant a new nature within us. We cannot have Christ Jesus as Savior and reject His Lordship, and this Biblical truth must be 'understood' from the beginning when the seed of the gospel is sown. We are called to 'make

64

disciples', not to offer Christ as a fire escape to those who desire to continue their life of sin. The Holy Spirit cannot be manipulated, and neither do we have the right to tell people that they are born again if they say some concocted sinner's prayer. Those who belong to Christ will be co-crucified with Christ; they will be filled with the Divine Nature and know their Master's voice.

Such disciples will put down strong roots and a solid foundation on which their lives will be built up and strengthened daily through both blessing and trials. They will daily come back to the cross and gaze upon its declaration of sacrifice and love, hold out open hands to their Lord who has the right to give and take away, trusting in Him and overflowing with thankfulness, dwelling daily in the living hope which testifies within their soul. They will accept God's gifts with joy, but hold them loosely in their hands for fear of loving the gift more than the giver, and in the knowledge that all that is Christ's is theirs as 'co-heirs' with Him.

Study Eleven

Super Apostles: Super Deceptions

Colossians 2: 8-10

8 See to it that no one takes you captive through hollow and deceptive philosophy, which depends on human tradition and the elemental spiritual forces of this world rather than on Christ.
9 For in Christ all the fullness of the Deity lives in bodily form,
10 and in Christ you have been brought to fullness. He is the head over every power and authority.

In this section Paul turns to the first of several warnings to the Colossians which identify the areas of danger to spiritual maturity in this Church. We do well to understand that Satan knows the gospel, perhaps better than most Christians. He knows that any person who has given their life to Christ unconditionally, and experienced regeneration, can never lose that salvation. His purpose of deceiving Christians is never to steal their soul, for this is impossible; rather, he determines to stop them from ever reaching spiritual maturity.

Paul opens this section with a military expression meaning to be 'carried away by an enemy' or 'kidnapped'. The idea here is that the one who has made a commitment to follow Christ on the narrow path will be diverted away from that path to one that leads to confusion, and halts effective spiritual growth. The weapon of the enemy in this case was 'hollow and deceptive philosophy', which had its basis in human traditions and demonic principles. Paul is not issuing a rebuke against all philosophy here, but a particular type of philosophy which has demonic roots. It is my conviction that similar forms of Gnostic philosophy, and its Eastern counterparts, are still present and increasing in congregations today. In this study we will look at some of those areas and at the 'human traditions' in the next study. In order to understand Paul's warnings about someone taking them captive, we will examine a similar situation in the Corinthian Church.

66

'Super-apostles'

In his second letter to the Corinthian Church the apostle Paul spends a great deal of the thirteen chapters defending his authority as an apostle. This situation came about after his first strong letter of rebuke regarding the abuses which were occurring in that church. In brief, Corinth was experiencing one of the lesser common forms of Gnosticism which developed out of its teachings on dualism. Gnostics separated the material and spiritual realms. Flesh was fundamentally evil and irredeemable, and spirit was good. In the Church at Colossae this teaching led to extreme forms of asceticism and 'harsh treatment of the body' (2:23), but at Corinth the opposite prevailed.

The Corinthians had fallen under the false teaching that no action in the body could have an effect on the spirit, and subsequently, this was the most carnal Church of the area. In 1st Corinthians chapter five we read of a man who is in a sexual relationship with his father's wife (5:1-2) and the Church was bragging about it. The woman was most likely his step-mother, but to the Corinthians, this man was taking this Gnostic philosophy to its extreme, a position that they considered made him even more 'spiritual' than pagans. In chapter six we read of men having sex with prostitutes. Paul reminds these ones that previously some of them had been male prostitutes and homosexuals, idolaters, adulterers, thieves, greedy, etc., (6:9-10), and he ends his discourse by telling them that their bodies are 'temples of the Holy Spirit' which should be used to honor God.

Paul's letter was met with resistance, especially amongst those leaders who considered themselves apostles of higher authority than him. They also demanded money for their services, an issue he spends much time talking about in his second letter.

The Corinthian Church had spiritual gifts in abundance, more so than any other mentioned in the New Testament, but it was also the most spiritually immature and divided. This was a church that placed a huge emphasis on experience, and little or none on spiritual discipline or solid Biblical theology. People were getting drunk on the communion wine at the Lord's Supper (11:22), indeed this was a church in which basically anything was permissible, for all was being done supposedly in the 'freedom of the spirit'. In his second letter, then, Paul writes these words in chapter 11;

4 For if someone comes and preaches a Jesus other than the one we preached, or if you receive a different spirit from the one you received, or a different gospel from the one you accepted, you put up with it readily enough. 5 But I do not think I am in the least inferior to those "super-apostles." 6 I may not be a trained speaker, but I do have knowledge. We have made this perfectly clear to you in every way.

There are powerful warnings to the Church of today. It is absolutely possible to be preaching a 'different Jesus'. Paul's warning here is against a Jesus of human creation, a Jesus that is presented in a way that suits the carnal natures of those who don't wish to walk the narrow path, a Jesus that doesn't talk about sin, about 'taking up our cross daily', and obeying Him. If the Jesus preached is not the Jesus of Scripture in all His Deity, Lordship and revelation, it is a different Jesus, and one who has no power to save or sanctify. Paul warned us that,

'the time will come when men will not put up with sound doctrine. Instead, to suit their own desires, they will gather around them a great number of teachers to say what their itching ears want to hear' (2nd Timothy 4:3).

When I hear the messages coming out of America and the West's mega Churches, messages that have diluted God's Word and replaced it with what people want to hear, I have no doubt that the time Paul was speaking of has arrived. Paul told Timothy to *'preach the Word; be prepared in season and out of season; correct, rebuke and encourage - with great patience and careful instruction'.*

All Christians, if we are to be honest, need correction, rebuke and encouragement, in all seasons; correction in any area of doctrine which contradicts the teaching of Scripture, rebuke for allowing our sin natures to dominate our lives, and encouragement to repent, accept forgiveness, and take our Lord's hand once more. If any of these are absent in the church you attend; if the gospel has been watered down to a point of powerlessness to sanctify you and prepare you for the tests of faith, then get to one which preaches reverently and faithfully the life-changing gospel of God's Word.

The second warning is about a 'different spirit'. The NASB version renders the verse clearer than the NIV stating 'or you receive a different spirit which you have not received'. There are two different words being used by the apostle which are translated as 'receive'; the first means to 'welcome and experience' and the second to 'judge or consider'. What Paul is saying is this. You welcome a different spirit which you have not judged or considered, have not discerned as a spirit other than the Holy Spirit. This is why the apostle mentions Satan deceiving Eve in the previous verse, for Paul believes that they have welcomed a demonic spirit to teach and lead them astray. Like the Colossians, they were 'being taken captive'.

The result is a 'different gospel' which is no gospel at all. These 'super-apostles', a title they took upon themselves, were also eloquent of speech, convincing and articulate, so much so that they criticized Paul for his simplistic message. Paul calls these men *'false apostles, deceitful workmen, masquerading as apostles of Christ', and not surprising because their master Satan masquerades as an angel of light* (11:13-14).

Some people believe that if an eloquent 'super-apostle' who performs signs and wonders does such things in the name of Jesus, then the spirit behind these things must automatically be the Holy Spirit. Christ and Paul (as we have seen) would disagree! The false teachers of Matthew 7:22-23 claimed to prophesy, drive out demons and perform miracles in Jesus' name, and Christ said He 'never knew them'. Jesus used a double negative when He spoke those words, meaning, 'I never ever knew you'. He calls them 'evildoers' and sends them away from His presence.

Over the past several decades the Western Church has become increasingly polarized. Many churches have moved away from solid theology in a quest for spiritual power and manifestations of power. Successful meetings are evaluated on the intensity and frequency of spiritual manifestations, rather than on 'correction, rebuke and encouragement' from God's Word, indeed, the Bible is scarcely opened in such meetings except to find a text to justify this lust for seeing 'miracles'. Jesus issued a grave warning to people who desired to live by sight rather than faith when He said that, 'an adulterous and wicked generation look for a sign' (Matthew 12:39, 16:4). Sight, not doubt, is the opposite of faith, and 'without faith it is impossible to please God' (Hebrews 11:6). Those who continually look for signs to bolster their flagging faith will remain spiritually immature.

On the other hand, there is a reaction against all things miraculous; indeed some churches declare that the gifts of the Spirit have ceased altogether. This reaction is equally unbiblical and comes from a fortress mentality. Wisdom comes from sound doctrine and balanced practice, always tested and approved by the Scriptures. The gifts of the Holy Spirit are never to be feared simply because counterfeits exist, rather, we are to exercise said gifts upon a mature foundation of God's Word, and be led by the Spirit as we test every spirit. The Church has always been, and will always be, under demonic spiritual attack until the Day of the Lord. A solid foundation of theology will question any new so-called 'move of the Holy Spirit' to see if it is a Biblical manifestation that produces lasting fruit in its recipients.

Paul's question to the Colossians and to us is really pretty simple. Is Jesus Christ absolutely and exclusively in the center of our worship? If a Church has exchanged Christ-centered teaching and worship with placing the Holy Spirit in the center, then alarm bells should be ringing out. The Holy Spirit will never allow Himself to be the center of worship (John 16), therefore, the 'spirit' that is accepting this position in meetings, which expect, demand and produce spiritual manifestations, is NOT the Holy Spirit of God. The bizarre manifestations of spiritual power, which have surfaced in many churches, have been around for thousands of years and are rooted in forms of Eastern religion such as Hinduism, and are practiced in Kundalini Yoga and many mystic religions.

Satan is all too willing to give gullible and immature people exciting mystical experiences in order to keep them in a state of spiritual immaturity. Like spoiled children who are never satisfied, many have an insatiable appetite for anything other than God's command to 'grow up'. Paul gave the Corinthians a final command in his second letter that we do well to heed in this day and age. 2nd Corinthians 13:5,

Examine yourselves to see whether you are in the faith; test yourselves. Do you not realize that Christ Jesus is in you - unless, of course, you fail the test.

70

Paul's point here is that if they pass the test and realize that Christ is indeed within them, they will understand that it is he, and his authority as an apostle, which has brought them to this place, and they will reject the Gnostic teachings of the false apostles. If they are indeed 'in Christ', then their emphasis must be on living *for* Christ, on 'putting off the sinful nature' (Colossians 2:11), and accepting the hardships and tests which refine and prove genuine faith.

To the Colossians, Paul points in exactly the same direction, the only direction we should ever look; namely to Christ and He alone.

'For in Christ all the fullness of the Deity lives in bodily form, and you have been given fullness in Christ, who is the head over every power and authority'.

Summary

Like many professing Christians today, the Colossians and Corinthians were seeking spiritual experiences rather, than simply walking in the Spirit through the ups and downs of life. They thought that there were higher and higher levels of spiritual power which manifested themselves in those who had discovered their mystical secrets. We see the same things today; wide-eyed, gullible people watching so-called spiritual leaders strutting up and down on stages performing acts of 'power' in Jesus' name. Do these 'leaders' ever teach solid Biblical exegesis, do they point to Christ and He alone, or rather call on the 'spirit' to manifest sign after sign while the gullible submit, seduced and deceived?

Spiritual maturity comes through years of submission to the cross of Christ, through holding His hand through hardships, through always keeping Him in the very center of our lives and allowing His transforming work. There is no shortcut, no mystical fast-track. There will be times of glorious celebration, times when He performs a miracle for His glory, times when we feel that He is close or far away, times of intercession and spiritual warfare, and times when we are just walking hand in hand with Him through a forest glade or on a sandy beach. But through all of these times we live in the reality that we have been given fullness in Christ and lack nothing.

Study Twelve

Human Traditions

Colossians 2: 11-23

Throughout the remaining part of chapter two Paul addresses the issue of legalism. Although the mystic element of Gnosticism was prevalent in Colossae, it is obvious from what follows in these verses that forms of Jewish legalism were also prevalent, albeit in a slightly different form to that which we find in Galatians. Keep in mind that Simon the Sorcerer, from whom Gnostic teachings came, was a Samaritan by birth. Simon's mother was a Jewess, and in the writings of Irenaeus, who confronted Gnosticism in detail, we see this thread of legalism which manifested itself in forms of self-development through obedience to rules and regulations.

In Corinth, the issue was extreme license to sexual immorality, but in Colossae the emphasis is on bodily discipline as the means to controlling the sin nature, and with help from supposed angelic revelation. In this study we will work through the passage verse by verse in an exegetic style.

[11] In him you were also circumcised with a circumcision not performed by human hands. Your whole self ruled by the flesh was put off when you were circumcised by Christ, [12] having been buried with him in baptism, in which you were also raised with him through your faith in the working of God, who raised him from the dead.

[13] When you were dead in your sins and in the uncircumcision of your flesh, God made you alive with Christ. He forgave us all our sins, [14] having cancelled the charge of our legal indebtedness, which stood against us and condemned us; he has taken it away, nailing it to the cross. [15] And having disarmed the powers and authorities, he made a public spectacle of them, triumphing over them by the cross.

Paul has just finished telling the Colossians that all the fullness of Deity lives in Christ and that they have fullness in Him. These next verses act as a bridge to the section on legalism which begins with the word 'therefore'. It is doubtful that conformity to circumcision was a major problem at Colossae, and Paul is using the practice more as a metaphor than rebuking 'Judaisers' for insisting on it as he does in Galatians. Paul's point is about death to self, and resurrection to new life in Christ by faith in Him. This is how we receive 'fullness in Christ', not by the means of discipline he is about to address.

Paul also paints a beautiful picture of Christ's work in fulfilling the Law with all of its rules and regulations. We were 'indebted' to keeping the Law, and yet could not cancel that debt. Christ in His death paid the debt owed, opening up the opportunity for us to be justified, declared 'not guilty' of sin. Christ took the written code and nailed it to the cross, covering it with His precious blood, a picture of the regenerating power of the new covenant. The old covenant was therefore rendered 'obsolete' (Hebrews 8:13) as the new covenant in Christ's blood came into effect.

We were dead in sins, but God made us alive with Christ, forgiving us all our sins, so that now we are no longer under condemnation (Romans 8:1-2). If Christians truly believed these promises, Paul would have had no need to write the next passages on legalism, for such is the all encompassing act of grace towards we who surrender our lives to Christ Jesus.

Christ 'triumphed' over the 'powers and authorities', a reference to Satan and the demons who serve him, by offering Himself as a perfect sacrifice for sin, as beautifully stated in Hebrews 2:14-15.

Since the children have flesh and blood, he too shared their humanity so that by his death he might destroy him who holds the power of death - that is, the devil - and free those who all their lives were in slavery by their fear of death.

Peter tells us (1st Peter 3:19-20) that Christ went down into Tatarus (hell) and declared His victory (preached) to the 'spirits' who disobeyed in the days of Noah. This is the only reference to Tatarus in Scripture, a place where the fallen angels who sinned with human women were chained until the Day of the Lord. The word 'preached' used here, is not to evangelize, but 'keruso', a word meaning to 'herald a victory' over an enemy. Satan's plan was to corrupt all of humanity and prevent the coming of the 'Seed', the Messiah, but Christ destroyed that plan.

Back to our exegesis of Colossians

16 Therefore do not let anyone judge you by what you eat or drink, or with regard to a religious festival, a New Moon celebration or a Sabbath day. 17 These are a shadow of the things that were to come; the reality, however, is found in Christ.

These verses indicate the side of Gnostic teaching which disguised itself in Jewish legalism. References to religious festivals, New Moon celebrations and the Sabbath Day are all taken from the traditions associated with Mosaic Law. The Gnostic's emphasis was on using such laws to gain higher states of spirituality through self-discipline, whereas in Galatians the teaching was that keeping the Law was essential for salvation. The former is happening here. Those who considered themselves super spiritual were insisting that these festivals and special days must be observed. They were judging those they considered less spiritual than themselves. Paul's point here is simple, the same point he makes throughout the entire letter.

Christ is all you need!

Everything that came before Christ is but a shadow of what has now come in Him; therefore, don't allow such judgments on yourself. There are some today who insist that the festivals, celebrations and details of Mosaic Law are to be observed by all Christians as a command of God; The Hebrew Roots Movement, 119 Ministries and the World Wide Church of God, to name a few. My view is that these movements are in error. Verses are quoted where Jesus tells us to keep His commandments, and verses like the one here in Colossians are twisted out of context to claim that Paul was stating that we should not let anyone judge us for *keeping* these festivals. Such an interpretation entirely misses the overall message of Colossians. This entire section is a list of actions and observances which Paul is refuting as neither necessary, nor useful in reaching spiritual maturity in Christ.

18 Do not let anyone who delights in false humility and the worship of angels disqualify you. Such a person also goes into great detail about what they have seen; they are puffed up with idle notions by their unspiritual mind. 19 They have lost connection with the head, from whom the whole body, supported and held together by its ligaments and sinews, grows as God causes it to grow.

20 Since you died with Christ to the elemental spiritual forces of this world, why, as though you still belonged to the world, do you submit to its rules: 21 "Do not handle! Do not taste! Do not touch!"? 22 These rules, which have to do with things that are all destined to perish with use, are based on merely human commands and teachings. 23 Such regulations indeed have an appearance of wisdom, with their self-imposed worship, their false humility and their harsh treatment of the body, but they lack any value in restraining sensual indulgence.

In verse 18 Paul mentions 'false humility and the worship of angels'. One of the fundamental issues regarding Gnosticism was the claim that secret knowledge was being communicated through angelic entities to the chosen few, and that these ones had risen above the others in spiritual awareness. These people went into 'great detail about what they had seen', and although they were trying to present themselves as humble recipients, Paul says they are 'puffed up' with spiritual pride. Paul's warning about disqualification does not relate to salvation, but rather rewards for living in and fulfilling God's will throughout our Christian life. As previously stated, Satan's goal is to seduce us away from the path that leads to spiritual maturity, and in doing so, effectively cancel our witness as 'light and salt', and deprive us of the rewards awaiting us.

Notice also the reference to Christ as the Head of the Body, and that such people have 'lost connection' with Christ. This verse links back to verse 17. The NIV translates 'however, the reality is found in Christ'. This certainly gives the heart of the point, but in the Greek text the same word 'body' is found as here in 18. Paul's point is to show the Colossians that the reality of Christ is found in being in the Body of Christ, in which we are all complete. Those who seek spiritual perfection outside of Christ have lost connection to Him as its Head. It is only in Him, Paul says, that the *'whole body, supported and held together by its ligaments and sinews, grows as God causes it to grow'*.

It is not in keeping festivals, Mosaic Laws or secret knowledge from angels that causes the individual parts of the Body of Christ to grow, but rather God. We are totally dependent on Him as ligaments, sinews etc., for our spiritual growth towards maturity. If someone has lost connection with the Head, repentance is necessary to restore the fellowship necessary to continue on to maturity (1st John 1: 6-9).

In verse 20 Paul brings us back to the foundation of our Christian lives as those who have been reborn, or born from above. We died with Christ, that is, our ego was crucified with Him (Galatians 2:20) and we became aliens and foreigners in this world, citizens of heaven (Philippians 3:20). The world system hates us because it does not know our Lord and Savior (John 17:13-19). Since we no longer belong to this world, why then do we feel an obligation to submit to its legalistic rules; *'Do not handle! Do not taste! Do not touch!'* Such rules are based on *'human commands and teachings'*, whereas the cry of the Christian is 'it is for freedom that Christ has set us free' (Galatians 5:1).

This last passage rebukes the Colossians for thinking that *'harsh treatment of the body'*, asceticism, can somehow make them more holy. Paul is not offering the Colossians a license for sensual indulgence through their freedom (Galatians 5:13), but telling them that sanctification comes from yielding to the Holy Spirit's sanctifying and transforming power, rather than legalistic and harsh bodily discipline.

According to his own testimony, Martin Luther, while he was still an Augustinian Monk, struggled with sensual thoughts and desires. The Roman Catholic Church taught that grace must be earned; therefore, a strict regime of prayer, meditation, fasting and penance was used to try and make one holy enough for God. Luther made himself a shirt of horsehair and wore it at night. If he was tormented by itching skin, the last thing on his mind would be sensual fantasies. He hoped that by such harsh treatment he would win God's favor and be able to feel His presence. At that time, Luther didn't realize that grace comes through faith in the saving power of Jesus Christ alone (Ephesians 2:8). Later, God revealed this truth to him and he was born again.

To believe that we can somehow make ourselves holy enough for God through self-discipline, is to insult the sacrifice of Christ in the extreme! At best it puts us on a performance trip, under the delusion that our relationship with Him depends solely on us, and at worst it insults the cross and Jesus' suffering as not being enough to satisfy God's wrath against sin.

When we have died with Christ we have a new nature within us, the Divine Nature, and therefore have no obligation to follow the desires of our sin nature (Romans 8:12). Rather, we make every effort to walk in the Spirit, turning our backs on sin, motivated by love for God because of his free gift to us, and never motivated by fear or the deception that somehow we can make Him love us more. This is Paul's point to the Colossians and to us.

In Summary

Up to this point in his letter, Paul has told the Colossians exactly who Jesus Christ is (1:15-20), their spiritual position in Him (1:21-23), and that Christ is the beginning and end of all the treasures of wisdom and knowledge. In the section we have just studied, he specifically attacks the various heretical teachings that are endangering the spiritual growth of this Church. We should not be surprised to realize that very similar heresies and claims of angelic visitations still abound in churches today, even amongst Protestants. Such heresies are thoroughly mixed into Orthodox Christianity where I serve the Lord in Ukraine, and of course within Roman Catholicism worldwide.

However, legalism has always been a problem in Protestant Churches, and in recent times this heretical idea of different levels of spiritual 'awareness' has surfaced. Yes, there are people who may be on a deeper level of spiritual maturity than especially new Christians, but this is not because they have secret knowledge or an angel giving them secret revelations. Spiritual maturity comes through obedience to the will of God, not obedience to regulations; and these are not the same thing! Legalism suggests that God's grace is limited to our performance and that we have to fill up what is lacking in Christ's sacrifice on the cross.

Even the most spiritual of us is sinful, and in my experience, those Christians who walk closest to their Savior are not puffed up about their maturity, but the most aware of their sinfulness and grateful for His perfecting power. Christ is all-sufficient! He alone is the author and perfector of our faith, the one who began a good work in us, the one who will, if we simply allow Him, will 'carry it on to completion' (Philippians 1:6).

Study Thirteen

Dead and Raised

Colossians 3: 1-4

3 Since, then, you have been raised with Christ, set your hearts on things above, where Christ is, seated at the right hand of God. ² Set your minds on things above, not on earthly things. ³ For you died, and your life is now hidden with Christ in God. ⁴ When Christ, who is your life, appears, then you also will appear with him in glory.

This short paragraph is a pivotal point in Paul's letter. It is a conclusion to all he has said before, and the foundation of all he is about to say. In these few words he shows the true alternative to the 'philosophy' of the false teachers. Paul has already mentioned dying with Christ (2:20) in his negative remarks about legalism, but here he begins with the positive counterpart.

Christians have already been co-resurrected with Christ. That statement may, for some, seem like empty theological jargon, but that should not be the case. Perhaps the reality of being raised with Christ is missing for some because the experience of dying with Christ is also lacking, and one must come before the other. Let's take a look at a more detailed explanation of this from Romans 6:1-14.

6 What shall we say, then? Shall we go on sinning so that grace may increase? ² By no means! We are those who have died to sin; how can we live in it any longer? ³ Or don't you know that all of us who were baptized into Christ Jesus were baptized into his death? ⁴ We were therefore buried with him through baptism into death in order that, just as Christ was raised from the dead through the glory of the Father, we too may live a new life.

⁵ For if we have been united with him in a death like his, we will certainly also be united with him in a resurrection like his. ⁶ For we know that our old self was crucified with him so that the body ruled by sin might be done away with, that we should no longer be slaves to sin— ⁷ because anyone who has died has been set free from sin.

⁸ Now if we died with Christ, we believe that we will also live with him. ⁹ For we know that since Christ was raised from the dead, he cannot die again; death no longer has mastery over him. ¹⁰ The death he died, he died to sin once for all; but the life he lives, he lives to God.

¹¹ In the same way, count yourselves dead to sin but alive to God in Christ Jesus. ¹² Therefore do not let sin reign in your mortal body so that you obey its evil desires. ¹³ Do not offer any part of yourself to sin as an instrument of wickedness, but rather offer yourselves to God as those who have been brought from death to life; and offer every part of yourself to him as an instrument of righteousness. ¹⁴ For sin shall no longer be your master, because you are not under the law, but under grace.

In this passage there are both statements of our position in Christ and challenges to us about that position. The message here is that he who is in Christ has 'died to sin' so that we 'may live a new life'. If that 'new life' isn't being manifested, we must honestly ask ourselves if death to sin has actually occurred. Christianity is not a set of nice ideas that we adopt, but rather a radical change in behavior through what has occurred existentially in the heart of our natures.

In verse 6 Paul says that *'we know that our old self was crucified with Him so that the body ruled by sin might be done away with, that we should no longer be slaves to sin'.*

If we are still slaves to sin, then where is the liberty we should be experiencing through the empowering of the Holy Spirit within us? Paul is never saying that our old natures will cease from desiring to sin; rather, he is stating that there will be within us a hatred for sin, implanted by God's presence within us, and the power to live a new life. We are to *'count ourselves dead to sin but alive to God in Christ Jesus. Therefore do not let sin reign in your mortal body so that you obey its evil desires'.*

If we have died with Christ and been raised with Him, we now have a choice regarding sin, whereas before being born again sin was ruling us, enslaving us. One of the marks of true conversion is this hatred for sin which the Divine Nature implants in our souls when He takes up residence within us. If we continue to let sin reign in our mortal bodies, we are either ignoring His inner call to holiness, or He is not within us at all!

Paul's answer to this problem is very simple;

'offer every part of yourself to him as an instrument of righteousness. [14] For sin shall no longer be your master, because you are not under the law, but under grace.'

This command echoes Jesus' words to 'take up our cross daily'. We come to the Lord and offer every part of ourselves as instruments of righteousness, for we have entered the Kingdom of Righteousness and are willing 'slaves (servants) of righteousness'.

'Just as you used to offer yourselves as slaves to impurity and to ever-increasing wickedness, so now offer yourselves as slaves to righteousness leading to holiness' (Romans 6:19).

As we saw in our previous study, we are not called to strict regimes of self-discipline, regulations and rules, but simply to *offer ourselves* every day. When we offer ourselves to the Lord we are making a conscious decision to live for Him that day. He will do the transforming work, and when temptations come throughout that day, we will not be taken unaware and yield to our sin natures and its desires, but rather, yield to His call and deprive our desire to sin. As we do this every day we grow in spiritual maturity and *'know we have been crucified with Christ'*.

Back to our text in Colossians.

...set your hearts on things above, where Christ is, seated at the right hand of God. [2] Set your minds on things above, not on earthly things.

Notice that Paul uses the word 'set' twice here; firstly concerning our hearts, and secondly our minds. The tense used here is about a daily conscious action, i.e., to continually set our hearts and minds on the things above. This focus on heavenly things is not automatic. We live busy lives where the mundane demands of life pull our focus down to earthly things. Paul told the Corinthians,

18 So we fix our eyes not on what is seen, but on what is unseen, since what is seen is temporary, but what is unseen is eternal (2nd Corinthians 4:18).

Paul is not suggesting that we must learn some balancing act as some suggest. The point here is about priorities and realities. The world tells us that our priorities must be about survival and saving/investing for the next generation. The world tells us that we are failures if we don't have a certain living standard, or leave wealth and financial security for our children. The world says that this life is the reality, the world we can see and have to live in, not the unseen future beyond the grave. Scripture never suggests we should be complacent about providing for our families, indeed Paul says in 1st Timothy 5:8 that,

8 anyone who does not provide for their relatives, and especially for their own household, has denied the faith and is worse than an unbeliever.'

We are commanded to live with a strong sense of family and social responsibility, indeed, this command is sown into the very fabric of Christian life. Jesus parable of the sheep and goats (Matthew 25), and others, underline this principle. However, we do all things in the knowledge that we are sojourners on this earth, just passing through, and our citizenship is in heaven. This is the reality we must instil, firstly into our own hearts and minds, and to our children. Those material things that God has given us, we hold loosely, guarding our hearts so that we do not fall in-love with the things of this world. We view our possessions as on loan from our Lord, things necessary to live as aliens here while we are 'light and salt' to those who are still dead to Christ. Paul summarizes this thought in verse 8.

'For you died, and your life is now hidden with Christ in God. 4 When Christ, who is your life, appears, then you also will appear with him in glory.

Here, then, is the reality of who we are. We have died and been raised with Christ. This new spiritual man is now hidden in Christ Himself who sits on the throne at the right hand of God. There are several vital points to grasp here.

Firstly: That the sin which enslaved and condemned us is hidden from the wrath of God, covered by the blood of Christ, therefore, when the Father looks upon us He sees His beloved Son. This is by no means a license to sin, rather a statement of grace which covers us throughout the remainder of our earthly lives as we *'put to death whatever belongs to our earthly natures'* (Colossians 3:5), because *'by one sacrifice he has made perfect forever those who are being made holy'* (Hebrews 10:14). In Christ, our perfection is completed, and until we receive our resurrection bodies, we are 'being made holy'. Such is the amazing gift of grace; to be declared and made perfect in Christ while we are becoming what we are declared to be.

Secondly: That Christ, being God, has His being in God, and likewise, we being in Christ have our being in God. This life is hidden in Christ and therefore secure in Him, unable to be touched or contaminated by anything or anyone because we are joined to Christ, in unity with Him eternally. This is one of the foundational doctrines of eternal security which is emphatic and non-negotiable. It is a beautiful picture of being covered by Christ, hidden beneath His wings, completely protected. Those who teach that there is no eternal security have no proper understanding of grace.

C. S. Lewis walked into a discussion about religion one evening and the question was raised; 'what is the difference between Christianity and every other religion'? "That's easy", he answered, "the answer is grace." Grace is God's 'unmerited favor'. Grace can never be earned, not by the most holy of persons, for *'all our righteousness is as a filthy rag'* (Isaiah 64:6). Grace is unmerited, unearned and absolutely undeserved; it is a gift to those who have entrusted their sinful lives to the Savior, a gift which is once and for all time.

Thirdly: Our new life in Christ is, to a certain extent, hidden from others and us. It becomes fully evident only when Christ, who is that life, appears in His glorious second coming. On that day when the Son of Man is revealed in all His glory, so too will those who are hidden in Him be revealed as sons and daughters of God, clothed like Christ in our resurrection bodies. Until then, we live in this sinful world, this perverted creation of God, the creation which will itself be redeemed, as Paul says: *'the creation waits in eager expectation for the sons of God to be revealed'* (Romans 8:19).

In Summary

Christianity is not a formula, ideal, or lifestyle choice which can be tacked on to our earthly ambitions and independence. It is a radical and total surrender to the will of God in Christ Jesus, which begins with placing our lives under His authority. When we do this, an existential death to self occurs which is validated by different manifestations which were not there previously. Two of these are hatred towards sin, and a desire for holiness. This change in attitudes happens because God's Spirit has taken up permanent residence within our souls. We now have two natures, human and Divine. One, the human, still desires to sin, and the other, the Divine, motivates and drives us to be holy. Since the Divine nature has destroyed the *power* of our slavery to sin, we now have a choice to say 'no' to our earthly desires and 'yes' to living a new life. Once we were slaves to sin, but now we are servants to righteousness.

The Christian life can be like a battle field, for a war rages within us as we grow towards spiritual maturity. Yet the answer to winning each battle is not in adding rules, regulations, traditions or trying to find secret spiritual shortcuts, rather, it is about 'offering ourselves to the Lord each day'. This is what Jesus meant when He said to 'take up our cross daily'. We began our walk with Christ at the foot of the cross, surrendering our egos to Him in the knowledge that we were slaves to sin. We walk each day in the same manner, only now, we have His power within us to win the battle against our old nature. Like all soldiers, sometimes we may lose a battle and be overwhelmed by sin. At such times we will hate ourselves for our weakness. This too is a mark of those who are truly born of God. The Christian cannot live with unconfessed sin in His life, he desires to be cleansed.

But we need not despair, for grace covers our weaknesses and motivates us to repent, get up, and keep walking with our Lord and Savior.

Study Fourteen

A New Direction

Colossians 3: 5-11

⁵ Put to death, therefore, whatever belongs to your earthly nature: sexual immorality, impurity, lust, evil desires and greed, which is idolatry. ⁶ Because of these, the wrath of God is coming. ⁷ You used to walk in these ways, in the life you once lived. ⁸ But now you must also rid yourselves of all such things as these: anger, rage, malice, slander, and filthy language from your lips. ⁹ Do not lie to each other, since you have taken off your old self with its practices ¹⁰ and have put on the new self, which is being renewed in knowledge in the image of its Creator. ¹¹ Here there is no Gentile or Jew, circumcised or uncircumcised, barbarian, Scythian, slave or free, but Christ is all, and is in all.

In this section there are several commands; 'put to death', 'rid yourselves', 'do not lie' and 'put on the new self'. On the surface of it, we may get the impression that we must have our eyes continually searching for signs of sin in our lives, be poised to eradicate any 'impurity, lust, evil desire or filthy language', and to avoid any circumstance that might induce feelings of 'anger, rage, malice', or temptation to 'slander or lie'. Sadly, some Christians live exactly this way, fall into the trap of legalism, or try to isolate themselves from the world. The problem with that is that we cannot be 'salt and light' in the world if we put walls around ourselves to keep the world away.

We are not called to be 'sin hunters', but rather, as we saw in the previous study, to 'set our hearts and minds on things above'. This does not mean to have our heads in the clouds or to be, as the saying goes, 'so heavenly minded that we are of no earthly use'. If we are forever concentrating on our sinful nature, we will miss the point entirely. The Scriptures teach us to concentrate our efforts and to set

85

our minds on the positive rather than the negative. Even the word 'repent' suggests exactly this. Repent means to turn 180 degrees, therefore, we are to turn our backs on sin and towards our new life in Christ, to go in a new direction. Look at these verses in 2nd Peter as an example.

3 His divine power has given us everything we need for a godly life through our knowledge of him who called us by his own glory and goodness. 4 Through these he has given us his very great and precious promises, so that through them you may participate in the divine nature, having escaped the corruption in the world caused by evil desires.
5 For this very reason, make every effort to add to your faith goodness; and to goodness, knowledge; 6 and to knowledge, self-control; and to self-control, perseverance; and to perseverance, godliness; 7 and to godliness, mutual affection; and to mutual affection, love. 8 For if you possess these qualities in increasing measure, they will keep you from being ineffective and unproductive in your knowledge of our Lord Jesus Christ. 9 But whoever does not have them is nearsighted and blind, forgetting that they have been cleansed from their past sins.
10 Therefore, my brothers and sisters, make every effort to confirm your calling and election. For if you do these things, you will never stumble, 11 and you will receive a rich welcome into the eternal kingdom of our Lord and Savior Jesus Christ.

Peter begins by telling us that *'His divine power has given us everything we need for a godly life through our knowledge of Him'*. That power lives within us for we have *'participated in the divine nature'*. After these words of encouragement, Peter does not tell us to go hunting for every evil thought or desire in order to eradicate it, rather, he tells us to *'make every effort to add to our faith goodness, knowledge, self-control, perseverance, godliness, mutual affection and love'*. The important issue here is about our focus. All of these qualities *'keep us from being ineffective and unproductive in our knowledge of our Lord Jesus Christ'*. And there, in a nutshell, is the key. All of these qualities increase as our knowledge of Christ increases. As we focus on Him, setting our hearts and minds on heavenly things, where He sits at God's right hand, all of these qualities grow as our knowledge and love for Him grows.

Peter then adds a warning, namely, that anyone who does not possess these qualities is *'nearsighted and blind and has forgotten they have been cleansed from past sins'*. The only way we could forget about our cleansing from past sins is if we have taken our eyes off Christ and the cross, if we have stopped 'taking up our cross'. Those who take their eyes off the cross of Christ soon become blinded by the world. Jesus told the Laodicean Church that they were 'wretched, pitiful, poor, blind and naked'. This Church boasted that it was wealthy and didn't need a thing, but He counselled them to buy 'gold refined in the fire' and 'salve to put on their eyes' (Revelation 3: 17-18). This Church made no effort to increase their knowledge of Christ, relying on their wealth, that which Paul calls 'idolatry' (Colossians 3:5). They were lukewarm; a condition that made God want to vomit.

Peter tells such people that they should *'confirm their calling and election'*, for it is the increase of godly qualities which is one of the manifestations of those who are born again. Keeping our eyes focused on Christ and the cross, and our hearts and minds on heavenly things, is the key to increasing in our knowledge of the Lord. If we do this, we will experience an increase in godly qualities.

But what about when sin overtakes us?

Hebrews 12:1 speaks of the sin which so easily entangles, and every Christian has experienced moments of weakness when our earthly nature has gotten the upper hand. 'Old habits die hard' and sometimes, if we take our eyes off the Lord, we can be easily entangled. At such times we can doubt our salvation, and certainly our spiritual enemy will try to fill our minds with condemnation and despair. How can we continue to sin if this old nature has been destroyed and raised again? Was it ever destroyed? The answer to that question is an emphatic 'no'. It is not our sin nature which has been destroyed, but rather the principle of sin rooted in our autonomous ego. It is extremely important for us to understand the difference!

Turn to 1st John chapter 3. In this chapter John begins with beautiful words of encouragement about how much God has lavished His love upon us. In verse 3 he says that *'everyone who has this hope in Him purifies himself, just as He is pure'*. So far, so good. But then in the following verses John makes statements which are very commonly misunderstood.

⁴ Everyone who sins breaks the law; in fact, sin is lawlessness. ⁵ But you know that he appeared so that he might take away our sins. And in him is no sin. ⁶ No one who lives in him keeps on sinning. No one who continues to sin has either seen him or known him.

⁷ Dear children, do not let anyone lead you astray. The one who does what is right is righteous, just as he is righteous. ⁸ The one who does what is sinful is of the devil, because the devil has been sinning from the beginning. The reason the Son of God appeared was to destroy the devil's work. ⁹ No one who is born of God will continue to sin, because God's seed remains in them; they cannot go on sinning, because they have been born of God. ¹⁰ This is how we know who the children of God are and who the children of the devil are: Anyone who does not do what is right is not God's child, nor is anyone who does not love their brother and sister.

In verse 4 John says that *'Christ came to take away sins'*. *'No one who lives in Him keeps on sinning'*, indeed, if we keep on sinning we have *'neither seen or known Him'*. These are very serious statements, but John reinforces them again. If we are righteous we do what is righteous, but if we are sinful we are still of the devil. Then he delivers a final blow in saying that *'no one who is born of God will continue to sin'*, *'they cannot continue to sin if they are born of God'*.

To those who misunderstand John's words in chapter 3, it would seem that none of us are born of God, born again. I have heard explanations of these verses from the sublime to the ridiculous, even pastors claiming that they never sin themselves and that it is possible, even expected, that Christians never commit sins. However, if this is the case, or even possible, it totally contradicts what John says in the first chapter of this same letter. See the following from chapter 1:5-10;

⁵ This is the message we have heard from him and declare to you: God is light; in him there is no darkness at all. ⁶ If we claim to have fellowship with him and yet walk in the darkness, we lie and do not live out the truth. ⁷ But if we walk in the light, as he is in the light, we have fellowship with one another, and the blood of Jesus, his Son, purifies us from all sin.

⁸ If we claim to be without sin, we deceive ourselves and the truth is not in us. ⁹ If we confess our sins, he is faithful and just and will forgive us our sins and purify us from all unrighteousness. ¹⁰ If we claim we have not sinned, we make him out to be a liar and his word is not in us.

And again in chapter 2;

2 My dear children, I write this to you so that you will not sin. But if anybody does sin, we have an advocate with the Father—Jesus Christ, the Righteous One. ² He is the atoning sacrifice for our sins, and not only for ours but also for the sins of the whole world.

It is absolutely obvious that John recognizes that Christians will commit sins, in fact, to claim that we don't is to call Jesus a liar. God forbid that we would make such a claim. John is never contradicting himself in chapter 3, rather, his words are completely misunderstood because he is speaking of two quite different things, the sin nature and the autonomous ego.

Let's go back to chapter 3. In verse 4 John tells us that 'sin is lawlessness'. This is the key to understanding everything he tells us after this statement. John is speaking of the root of sin, and this is why he mentions Satan in verse 8. The root of sin is rebellion against God, a refusal to submit to God's rule over our lives. Satan was the first to rebel, and continues in his rebellion. The principle of sin is the ego of the creature standing with a raised fist against our Creator demanding our independence and autonomy.

Here, then is the difference between Christian and non-Christian. The Christian is one who has submitted their egoistic autonomy to the will of God, has submitted to Christ's authority as Lord. The non-Christian still refuses to submit, like Satan, he sits on the throne of his own life. Earlier we asked the question, 'has our old nature been destroyed'? The answer is 'no' it hasn't, and the Scriptures never say otherwise. What was destroyed in us was our autonomous ego and the Scriptures declare this as in Galatians 2:20-21.

²⁰ I have been crucified with Christ and I no longer live, but Christ lives in me. The life I now live in the body, I live by faith in the Son of God, who loved me and gave himself for me. ²¹ I do not set aside the grace of God, for if righteousness could be gained through the law, Christ died for nothing!"

The word 'I' in Greek is ego, but the ego and sin nature are two different things. Our egos have been co-crucified with Christ; therefore, we no longer refuse to submit to the will of God. John is saying exactly this in chapter 3. No born again Christian can ever commit the sin of lawless rebellion because his ego is crucified with Christ. His sin nature still exists, and when he commits sins in his body, he gets on his knees and repents, whereas the non-Christian refuses to repent. John's words in chapter 3 should be an encouragement to all born again Christians. One of the proofs that we are truly God's children is that we obey John's words in the previous chapters, i.e., when we sin we confess our sins and seek forgiveness.

In Summary

All Christians go through weak moments in our lives and become entangled in sin. Our sin nature remains in us after we are born of God, and although we may wish He had destroyed this ugly part of us at new birth, God in His wisdom leaves it within us, perhaps to show us how much we need to rely on His grace and power, perhaps also to prevent us from becoming proud and to help us to empathize with those who still need salvation. But is it not also in the battle against sin that we prove our love for Jesus Christ, the love that He so dearly cherishes?

But we do well to remember *that 'if anyone does sin, we have one who speaks to the Father in our defence - Jesus Christ, the Righteous One'.* He calls us to *'confess our sins'* and He is *'faithful and just and will forgive us our sins and purify us from all unrighteousness'.* John's letter was written to those he called his 'dear children', Christians, but his words were always to encourage, and never condemn. It is important, therefore, to believe that when we sincerely seek forgiveness, that we have been purified. The greater sin is to disbelieve we have been forgiven, for disbelief dilutes the Lord's sacrifice on the cross as if His sacrifice cannot cover all sin.

Don't become a 'sin hunter', but rather turn your back on sin and deprive your old nature. Feed your soul on Christ Jesus, keeping your eyes on the cross and setting your heart and mind on heavenly things.

As you do this, the godly qualities which confirm your calling and election will increase, and you will understand that you've *'taken off your old self with its practices* [10] *and have put on the new self, which is being renewed in knowledge in the image of its Creator.*

Study Fifteen

Living as The Chosen

Colossians 3: 12-17

12 Therefore, as God's chosen people, holy and dearly loved, clothe yourselves with compassion, kindness, humility, gentleness and patience. 13 Bear with each other and forgive one another if any of you has a grievance against someone. Forgive as the Lord forgave you. 14 And over all these virtues put on love, which binds them all together in perfect unity.

15 Let the peace of Christ rule in your hearts, since as members of one body you were called to peace. And be thankful. 16 Let the message of Christ dwell among you richly as you teach and admonish one another with all wisdom through psalms, hymns, and songs from the Spirit, singing to God with gratitude in your hearts. 17 And whatever you do, whether in word or deed, do it all in the name of the Lord Jesus, giving thanks to God the Father through him.

In the previous passage Paul gave us two lists of five vices which Christians are to 'rid themselves of'. In this passage he lists five virtues which Christians are to 'clothe' themselves with. We understand that the grace of God in Christ covers our sins whilst the indwelling Spirit guarantees our inheritance (Ephesians 1:14), yet we are also called to 'make every effort to 'add to our faith (2nd Peter 1:5-6) the virtues which show us to be 'God's chosen people'. The terms 'chosen, holy and dearly loved' echo the special titles given in the Old Testament (Isaiah 43:20, 65:9) to Israel as God's own possession, a term used also of the Church in Ephesians 1:14 and of Christ in Luke 23:35.

Paul is showing our similarities to Israel and Christ in order to encourage us to behave in a Christlike way. Our motivation is never out of fear of losing our salvation and coming under God's wrath, for Jesus Christ has cancelled the debt against us. We, as God's chosen people, His adopted children, are 'dearly loved' by Him for the sake of Christ who has cleansed us. Paul desires that we grasp the depth of how much we are loved, so that love, and love alone, will be the driving force which motivates us to apply love in all its forms; compassion, kindness, humility, gentleness and patience. We are urged to dress ourselves in these virtues, putting them on each day like articles of clothing which are obvious to all who see us.

The virtues listed are used elsewhere in Scripture as characteristics of God or Christ, and show that as God's elect we should reflect the same. Several of these are also listed in the fruits of the Spirit (Galatians 5:22) where Paul encourages Christians to be led by and live by the Holy Spirit, rather than gratifying the old sinful nature.

In verse thirteen we are commanded to 'bear with and forgive one another'. Paul refers to having a grievance with other Christians, and his intention is to encourage 'perfect unity' among believers. The word Paul uses for 'forgive' literally means to cancel a debt, the same word Jesus uses in Luke 7:42 in His parable of the two debtors. That parable was told to a judgmental Pharisee who was staring arrogantly at a prostitute (probably Mary Magdalene) weeping on Jesus feet. Jesus' purpose was to get this man to look at his own heart, rather than judging one who desired to have her heart cleansed. Jesus warning in Matthew 6:14-15 has a similar message, that if we refuse to forgive others, neither will we be forgiven.

The fundamental issue here is about pride, and pride is detestable to God. Paul points us to Christ Himself and echoes Jesus' words to 'forgive as the Lord forgave you'. There will be countless times when people grieve us, both intentionally and unintentionally. At such times we are to remember how often we have done the same to others, even to God Himself, and rather than stand in indignant judgment, we are to do unto others as Christ has done unto us, namely, cancel the debt and forgive.

Jesus spoke of how we point out a speck in our brother's eye and ignore the plank in our own. It is our pride first and foremost which brings disunity. All of us have a fallen nature which can lead us into various forms of sin against our Lord and others. When we are tempted to judge rather than forgive, let us remind ourselves of the myriad times we have knelt in repentance before our Lord since we were saved.

Also, understand that there is a great deal of difference between forgiving a grievance and having theological disputes. When it comes to making judgments about doctrines we are called to use wisdom and humility, recognizing that we are the 'body' of Christ in which we collectively discern truth with the help of the Holy Spirit and Scripture. Yes, there are fundamental and non-negotiable doctrines on which we must never compromise, but destroying unity in the body over trivial matters dishonours Jesus Christ and the unity He commands us to have. I have heard people call each other heretics, fools, deceived, and other names, over whether or not they believe in a pre-tribulation or post-tribulation rapture, and even if they believe in the Rapture at all. Such behavior is utterly foolish and non-christlike.

If someone denies the Divinity of Christ, that salvation is by grace through faith, that God is triune in nature, or any other fundamental doctrine of Christianity, we can have no unity with this person, for it is unlikely they know Jesus Christ at all. But again, we are to make every effort to help them find Christ, rather than arrogantly argue our point. We were all ignorant of truth, blinded by 'the god of this age' at one stage, and arrogant Christians only made us raise our defences higher. We are called to be 'salt and light', not a battering ram.

14 And over all these virtues put on love, which binds them all together in perfect unity.

In this verse Paul continues his language of putting on clothes. Love is to be the outermost garment that covers all others. This virtue binds all others together in perfect unity, and by its humble nature, love brings this unity to the Body of Christ. If we Christians would just clothe ourselves in such a way, would we not make a far greater influence for our Lord in this world and dissolve those differences which are unimportant?

15 Let the peace of Christ rule in your hearts, since as members of one body you were called to peace. And be thankful.

The peace which Paul speaks of here has a several meanings. Firstly, it is Christ's peace, that peace which He embodies as the Lord of Peace, as in Ephesians 2:14 where He brings reconciliation both between individuals and God, and between the recipients of the first and new covenants. In Christ these barriers are destroyed.

94

Secondly, He brings the peace which is our salvation. Previously we were at war with God and subjects of His wrath, but in Christ that war is over. The same peace He has with the Father is our peace. Thirdly, Paul says that Christ's peace must 'rule' in the midst of the Church. He is to control every area of our lives as we relate to one another, for when we were saved we were called into this peace. For all of these reasons Paul tells us to be thankful.

[16] *Let the message of Christ dwell among you richly as you teach and admonish one another with all wisdom through psalms, hymns, and songs from the Spirit, singing to God with gratitude in your hearts.*

The *message* or *word* of Christ Paul refers to here is the gospel of the Kingdom which centres on Christ and our inheritance in Him. Christ's message called us to Him, brought peace as we surrendered to Him, and continues to transform and teach us as we yield to Him through the empowering of the Holy Spirit within us. We are called to teach and warn each other in a wise and holy way, recognizing that no individual has or will be given absolute revelation; rather, we must listen to one another in humility, and warn each other in that same spirit of recognition of our own weaknesses.

This teaching takes place in an attitude of worship and gratitude to God, accompanied by Spirit-inspired psalms, hymns and spiritual songs, a broad expression for the variety of Christian praise and worship music. Paul's parallel thoughts in Ephesians 5: 19-20 show his meaning even clearer, where he tells us to 'make music from our hearts to the Lord', a beautiful way of describing the joy of celebrating our salvation in, and love for the Lord.

[19] *speaking to one another with psalms, hymns, and songs from the Spirit. Sing and make music from your heart to the Lord,* [20] *always giving thanks to God the Father for everything, in the name of our Lord Jesus Christ.*

Paul's final remarks cover every aspect of our lives.

[17] *And whatever you do, whether in word or deed, do it all in the name of the Lord Jesus, giving thanks to God the Father through him.*

'Whatever' we do must be done in obedience to the Lord and in honor of His name, and be accompanied by thanksgiving to God. Not only are we to be thankful for what God has done *for* us, but also thankful for what He does *through* us. Our 'words and deeds', when surrendered to the Lord, are done in His name and power. Without Him we can achieve nothing of value in His kingdom in which we live, therefore, we live in gratitude that we are co-heirs in the work that He has called us to. This is what it means to live as the chosen.

Study Sixteen

Instructions to Wives

Colossians 3: 18-19

18 Wives, submit yourselves to your husbands, as is fitting in the Lord. 19 Husbands, love your wives and do not be harsh with them.

These verses have often been taken out of context, along with similar passages on the same topic, throughout Church history, therefore, in order to get a broader picture of God's ideal for marriage we will use the more comprehensive passage in Ephesians 5: 21-33. It is likely that that Colossians and Ephesians were written within a few days of each other, and Paul intended that both letters would be read by both congregations.

Ephesians 5:21. Submit to one another out of reverence for Christ. 22 Wives, submit yourselves to your own husbands as you do to the Lord. 23 For the husband is the head of the wife as Christ is the head of the church, his body, of which he is the Savior. 24 Now as the church submits to Christ, so also wives should submit to their husbands in everything.

In our last study we saw that Paul moves from the idea of making music in our hearts to the Lord, to the summary verses for husbands and wives. He uses the exact same pattern here in Ephesians. Please notice that I have included verse 21 into the section on marriage, however, although this verse begins with the word 'submit' in the NIV, in the original it is part of the previous sentence as in *'always giving thanks to God the Father for everything, in the name of our Lord Jesus Christ, and submitting to one another out of reverence for Christ'*. In its original context, then, it is tied to a general command for Christians to submit to each other, and continues into the passage on marriage.

Every Christian is called to 'submit to one another out of reverence for Christ', no matter our position, gifting, or place of authority in the Church. This is the heart of servanthood and the mark of any true leader. Christ submitted all to the will of the Father, even submission to death as a servant and sacrifice. We are all called to do the same. This attitude must be the foundation upon which Christian marriage is grounded.

Having said that, however, the verb used (submit) is a military word meaning to understand and obey a chain of command. In our modern thinking the idea of a hierarchy of command in the Church may be repulsive to many, but it is the language Paul uses. Obviously, we can argue that there are echoes of social and cultural practices in play here, and no doubt this is true, however, there are also important spiritual reasons for this spiritual hierarchy which we do well to consider.

Later in this passage Paul quotes Genesis, so we can assume he is recalling the Fall in his commands regarding submission within marriage. His command to wives concerns headship; the husband is the head of the wife as Christ is the head of the Church. Headship is never about a form of dictatorial authority; if that were so, Paul would never use Christ as his example. Rather, the idea Paul wants to express concerns a form of spiritual protection, in the sense of a spiritual umbrella. We can see Paul's thinking on this in 1st Timothy 2: 11-14 where he prohibits women to have spiritual authority over men. His argument is that Eve was the one deceived, rather than Adam, reminding his readers of the Fall.

In practical terms, what does that mean, and why should Eve's mistake and rebellion be used as a precedent for all women to be under their husband's spiritual authority? We might also ask why Satan chose Eve to seduce rather than Adam? I sincerely believe that the answer to all of these questions is in recognizing some of the profound differences in genders. When referring to salvation, there is 'no longer male or female', but in terms of communicating with the spiritual world, history has proven without doubt that women are far more susceptible to demonic seduction than men. I speak very generally here, not to specific individuals.

In terms of those involved in witchcraft, clairvoyance, horoscopes, New Age religions, channelling, using crystals, mysticism, etc., about 90% are women. Women also have a form of 'intuition' which is completely foreign to men. In general terms, then, compared to women, men are spiritual drones, and in that sense, more suitable to warding off demonic seduction. In the Church at Colossae, it was women leading the charge in worshipping angels, and Gnosticism in general was a form of mysticism dominated by women.

Is there a case, therefore, to argue that Satan recognizes that a woman who steps out from under her husband's spiritual protection is fair game, and that this is basically what Eve did? And is this the reason that God has instituted a hierarchy of spiritual authority which stems straight back to His command to Eve in Genesis 3:16 that, her 'husband would rule over her'. Although we are discussing this topic from both old and new covenants, it seems to me that there is a spiritual principle here which is consistent with both. The Church is under the spiritual authority and protection of Christ, the husband is under Christ's headship, and the wife under her husband's spiritual protection as unto the Lord. If this is indeed the Lord's chain of spiritual authority, then we put ourselves in the sights of the enemy if we rebel against it.

In 1st Corinthians 11:2-16 we read Paul's instructions concerning head coverings within a Christian meeting. Most interpreters would agree that Paul is addressing a predominately cultural issue here, namely, that Corinthian prostitutes, of which there were a great number, used their uncovered hair to advertise their trade. In that culture a woman's hair was a sign of sexuality, and Paul was adamant that Christian women should never draw attention to their physical beauty. However, I believe that there was another issue at stake which Paul alludes to in verse 10 of this chapter where he writes:

For this reason, and because of the angels, the woman ought to have a sign of authority on her head.

Two interpretations are given for this verse, both of which most likely apply. The first concerns the sin of fallen angels from Genesis 6:2 where angels were seduced by the beauty of women, taking them as wives and producing the Nephilim who brought demonic practices into the world. It was this act which triggered the absolute corruption of humanity culminating in the flood. Was Paul telling Christian women not to tempt angels?

Secondly, the head covering was a 'sign of spiritual authority', meaning, that a wife was publically declaring that she considered herself under her husband's spiritual authority and, therefore, protection. The thought here is that fallen angels would have no opportunity to attack, seduce, and use this woman to corrupt the Church, for the creature would be forced to go through the husband to get to her.

The chain of command God has instituted is like layers of spiritual protection. Christ stands as the first line of defence, the husband is under Christ's authority, and the wife under his authority 'as if under the Lord'. If either husband or wife steps out from under Christ's authority, fallen angels have the opportunity to deceive, seduce, and use such people to cause disunity and bring heresy into the Body of Christ.

Many women may feel resistance to this chain of authority, believing mistakenly that it puts husbands in a position of power which is unacceptable. This is a completely false assumption; indeed, the reality is quite the opposite. Let's examine a biblical example in a story about Abraham and Sarah. In 1st Peter 3:1-7 the apostle addresses the issue of submission, relating examples of women from Old Testament times and tells us that;

'They were submissive to their own husbands, like Sarah, who obeyed Abraham and called him her master. You are her daughters if you do what is right and do not give way to fear'.

Now turn to Genesis 12:10-20 and read a story of the power of a women (Sarah) who submitted 'as unto the Lord', a woman who didn't 'give way to fear', but trusted God.

[10] Now there was a famine in the land, and Abram went down to Egypt to live there for a while because the famine was severe. [11] As he was about to enter Egypt, he said to his wife Sarai, "I know what a beautiful woman you are. [12] When the Egyptians see you, they will say, 'This is his wife.' Then they will kill me but will let you live. [13] Say you are my sister, so that I will be treated well for your sake and my life will be spared because of you."

[14] When Abram came to Egypt, the Egyptians saw that Sarai was a very beautiful woman. [15] And when Pharaoh's officials saw her, they

praised her to Pharaoh, and she was taken into his palace. ¹⁶ He treated Abram well for her sake, and Abram acquired sheep and cattle, male and female donkeys, male and female servants, and camels.

¹⁷ But the LORD inflicted serious diseases on Pharaoh and his household because of Abram's wife Sarai. ¹⁸ So Pharaoh summoned Abram. "What have you done to me?" he said. "Why didn't you tell me she was your wife? ¹⁹ Why did you say, 'She is my sister,' so that I took her to be my wife? Now then, here is your wife. Take her and go!" ²⁰ Then Pharaoh gave orders about Abram to his men, and they sent him on his way, with his wife and everything he had.

Imagine being in Sarah's position here. Abraham has told a half truth about his wife in order to save his own skin. Sarah was his half-sister, yet he basically commanded his wife to be included in this deception. Sarah obeyed, and when the most powerful king in the known world saw her beauty, decided to take her for himself. It was customary for a woman to go through a time of preparation, weeks and often months, so Sarah is separated from her husband and knows she is going to be given to another man, basically forcing her into a position of adultery. Abraham is silent about it and happily accepts a great deal of gifts from Pharaoh. He seems to be more interested in saving his own skin than the integrity of his wife or sanctity of their marriage. There's no doubt in my mind that Sarah would have been praying about this situation, although the text doesn't say.

However, God acts on her behalf. Keep in mind that Pharaoh considered himself a god and had no belief in the God of Abraham. But *the Lord inflicted serious diseases on Pharaoh and his household **because** of Abram's wife Sarah.* Basically, God was telling this despot, 'this woman honors me by obeying her husband...touch her and die'.

God honored Sarah and rescued both she and her weak husband from the clutches and anger of the Egyptian king. Sarah could have rebelled against Abraham. We might say that she had every right to, for he was including her in a deception and lie that was leading her unwillingly into another man's bed. But this woman decided to trust the Lord even in this dire situation. If she had rebelled against Abraham, and God, perhaps her husband might have been killed. She chose to hold onto her faith in God's command to her, despite her husband's lack of faith at the time, and God honored her faith.

101

Sarah did not give way to fear even when her husband forced her to join in a deceitful lie. On this occasion, Abraham was out of God's will, but Sarah saved the day on account of her faith in remaining under the spiritual authority of her husband. The lie was Abraham's, not hers.

There is a great lesson here for all of us, but especially for Christian wives, namely, that God honors those who trust Him and hold onto His promises by faith, even in the most trying circumstances. Sarah understood that her role was to obey her husband as unto the Lord. She could have rebelled against that spiritual authority, and if so, perhaps the outcome would have been very different. Instead, she chose to trust God's command to her and honor that command. In turn, the Lord honored her and rescued the family.

Whether or not Sarah was aware of it, her position of obedience was not one of weakness to a weak husband, but rather, one of power in having God fight on her behalf, for her position was one of truth in remaining under spiritual authority. God's chain of command must be devoid of the 'what ifs' that compromise it. "What if my husband is teaching heresies, what if he commands me to do something which is against God's Word"? Sarah, and the Lord who honored her, answer those questions for us.

The challenge for 21st century Christian wives is often culturally influenced. Secular society has no understanding of the spiritual values of faith, no inkling of the way that God stands as guardian of His commands to those who trust Him. The secular world would have told Sarah to stand up for her feminist rights or dump her weak husband, and sadly, some within the Church would give similar advice, saying that God would never ask a wife to submit to a liar, heretic or weak leader. The woman of faith turns her back on such advice and trusts in the promises of God, in the leading of Christ, submitting to her husband as unto the Lord, and in doing so, invoking the power of God on her behalf for the sake of truth.

Be like Sarah and 'don't give in to fear' or stand in judgment over your husband's weakness, using it as an excuse to rebel. Trust the Lord and let Him judge your situation and come to your rescue.

Remember that every Christian is under a chain of spiritual authority within the Body of Christ. This does not mean that we do not admonish and correct those who are teaching or practicing falsehood. God has instituted authority to elders and such to judge heresy etc., even to remove pastors and teachers, but each of us must clearly understand our place in that chain of command and remain in it, trusting the Lord to be the Head of the Church.

In marriage, the role of wives is clearly stated. It is not a position of weakness, as Sarah demonstrated, but one of partnership with Christ and her husband. In our next study we will examine the role of husbands.

Study Seventeen

Instructions to Husbands

Colossians 3: 18-19

As in our last study, we will be using Paul's teaching from Ephesians 5:21-33 to get a comprehensive view of the roles of husbands and wives in Christian marriage. In this study we are looking at the role of husbands. Firstly, some thought about the word 'submission'.

Submission

Please notice again that I am beginning the study from verse 21 of Ephesians 5. There were no chapter and verse distinctions when Paul wrote this letter. Some may teach that the words *submit to one another out of reverence for Christ'* belong exclusively to the previous verses, but this would be inconsistent with the way Paul writes. Verse 22 begins with 'wives submit to your husbands', therefore, Paul's keyword for his new topic is the verb 'submit'. It was a very common literary device to make a summary statement and then unpack it into categories; indeed, the very first verse of the Bible opens this way, telling us that God created the heavens and the earth, and then the details of the creation process over the next verses. This is exactly what the apostle is doing here, therefore, the 'submit to one another' is Paul's summary command, and what follows are the detailed roles of submission.

As mentioned in our previous study, God has put in place a hierarchy of spiritual authority, not one of dictatorship. The Lord is the head of this hierarchy, a position He has earned through His servant heart and total submission to the will of the Father (Philippians 2: 5-11). As the Body of Christ we are to submit to one another, and this command includes husbands and wives. The wise Christian husband submits to his wife as the person to whom he is 'one flesh', seeking her wisdom in partnership and love out of reverence to Christ. This never means putting her in a place of spiritual authority over himself and the family, for that would leave her in a vulnerable position in regards to demonic attack.

Consider this example. A young single woman who has a passion for ministry goes to a Bible college and gains a degree in theology. She is recognized by her leaders and peers as having leadership gifts, especially in the areas of teaching. She marries a quiet and gentle man who is gifted in administration and service ministries. Some Churches would deny this woman the opportunity to use her teaching gift out of a misinterpretation of God's intention in the hierarchy of spiritual authority. When the Lord says through Paul that a woman must not have 'authority' over a man, He means exactly that, not that she cannot use her gift under *her husband's* authority. The situation we have described would seldom happen in Paul's day, yet there are examples of women leaders in the Early Church. These woman used their God-given gifts, but always in submission to their husband's spiritual authority, or if single, the authority of the Church's elders.

The wise husband recognizes his wife's spiritual gifts and encourages her to use them under the protection of his God-given spiritual protection/authority, both for *his* benefit and those who are taught by her. But a word of warning. All of us retain our old fallen nature and can be deceived by our ego. It is but a small step out from under that spiritual umbrella, both for women in regards to husbands, and men in regards to elders and other Church leaders. Therefore, Paul's first command to 'submit to one another out of reverence to Christ' must always be foremost in our minds. Having said that, let's read Paul's instructions to husbands from Ephesians 5: 28-28.

25 Husbands, love your wives, just as Christ loved the church and gave himself up for her 26 to make her holy, cleansing her by the washing with water through the word, 27 and to present her to himself as a radiant church, without stain or wrinkle or any other blemish, but holy and blameless.

28 In this same way, husbands ought to love their wives as their own bodies. He who loves his wife loves himself. 29 After all, no one ever hated his own body, but he feeds and cares for it, just as Christ does the church— 30 for we are members of his body.

31 "For this reason a man will leave his father and mother and be united to his wife, and the two will become one flesh." 32 This is a

*profound mystery — but I am talking about Christ and the church. 33
However, each one of you also must love his wife as he loves himself,
and the wife must respect her husband.*

Love

The primary command to husbands is in the word 'love'. There
are several words for different forms of love within Scripture,
including *eros* (erotic love), but the word used throughout this passage
is *agape*, that which is described in detail in 1st Corinthians 13,
therefore, Paul is not commanding husbands regarding romance, but
godly character and actions.

It is very noticeable that the apostle Paul relates this entire
passage to husbands through the lens of Christ and the Church, rather
than from Genesis 3. He never says 'husbands rule your wives as is
your right since Eve fell first to temptation'. The culture in which
Ephesians was written was primarily a patriarchal one, so I would
suggest that Paul is deliberately excluding from his instructions any
hint of autocratic rule within the family. Indeed, Paul's entire
emphasis to husbands is to have the servant attitude of Christ, an
attitude which manifests itself in acts of love.

Paul uses language relating to Christ's transforming work in the
body of Christ. As Christians we are joined to Christ in His body. In a
similar, yet mysterious way, husbands and wives are joined through
the 'one flesh' principle he alludes to in verses 31-32. This is the only
time Paul quotes Genesis, but his point is that, although husbands and
wives are individual believers in regards to salvation, their marriage is
a holy institution, a mysterious spiritual joining into the image of God
in Christ. Just as we are mysteriously joined to Christ as His spiritual
'body', so too are husbands and wives joined spiritually.

*25 Husbands, love your wives, just as Christ loved the church and
gave himself up for her 26 to make her holy, cleansing her by the
washing with water through the word, 27 and to present her to himself
as a radiant church, without stain or wrinkle or any other blemish, but
holy and blameless.*

In a Christian marriage a husband should never see himself as a
ruling authority which makes the family holy through his spiritual

authority, rather, in the same way 'as Christ', he must 'give himself up' for the sanctifying of his family. Christ gave Himself up for the sake of the Church. Some have mistranslated the meaning of these words to suggest that a man's primary commitment is to be willing to die in defence of his family as Christ died for the Church. Although a man must always be ready to protect his family, this is not the intention of the passage. Christ gave Himself up by emptying Himself of Divine authority ((Philippians 2:7). He became a servant/slave for the purpose of presenting those who would believe perfect to God. Husbands are called to the same role as servant/slaves under the Lord's authority and example; such is Paul's use of the command 'in the same way'. Therefore, the husband's role is to be the primary sanctifying influence in his family, under the sanctifying authority of the Lord, and in the same servant attitude of the Lord.

Just as Christ presents His bride the Church as holy and radiant, without stain, blemish or wrinkle, so husbands and wives present their marriage in the same way to Him.

28 In this same way, husbands ought to love their wives as their own bodies. He who loves his wife loves himself. 29 After all, no one ever hated his own body, but he feeds and cares for it, just as Christ does the church— 30 for we are members of his body.

Just as Christ cares for His bride, so too husbands must care for theirs. Christ loves His body the Church, and a man must love his body, the marriage. Husbands and wives are joined as 'one flesh' in a similar way to the Church being joined to Christ. Paul makes this point very clear in verses 31-32 as he relates the one flesh principle in marriage to our being joined in Christ.

31 "For this reason a man will leave his father and mother and be united to his wife, and the two will become one flesh." 32 This is a profound mystery — but I am talking about Christ and the church. 33 However, each one of you also must love his wife as he loves himself, and the wife must respect her husband.

The overarching principle in all of this teaching is that husbands are to be Christlike in the way they serve Christ within the structure of the family. That in itself is a very tall order, one which will require frequent self-examination, humility, wisdom, sacrifice, and also support from their wives.

33 However, each one of you also must love his wife as he loves himself, and the wife must respect her husband.

Paul's summary statement brings the entire passage into focus. Paul's statement to a husband to 'love his wife as he loves himself' covers all of the principles we have just discussed. This love cares for the physical body through manifestations of love through loving actions. As the husband practices loving action, love is manifested as the principle on which the marriage is built.

In my ministry as a pastor I often have young Christian couples visit me for counselling advice, a role I am not particularly comfortable with or trained for. Often these couples are such that I have had little input into their lives previously, and they are unaware of the principles I teach for Christian marriages. All too often the problem goes something like this. They believed themselves passionately in love and for the first year or two everything has gone well. Then they have been blessed with a child and the dynamics have changed radically. Ukraine has a quite traditionally patriarchal view of marriage. Men are seen as the primary bread winners, and seldom venture into the kitchen, indeed, many men have never cooked a meal for their families, made beds, washed and ironed clothes etc. With the new baby, the young mother is constantly tired and trying to find the energy to be romantic is difficult. As time goes on intimacy becomes increasingly rare.

What I find so common in such couples, and older more experienced couples, is this; the wife's love for her husband has transformed to a different form of love, whereas the husband is still operating on the more superficial love of eros. If I ask the woman if she loves her husband, the reply is almost always yes. Husbands, however, feel that those 'feelings' have basically died. He may tell me how he buys perfume and flowers, etc., but this just doesn't work anymore. At this point I generally ask to speak to the husband privately and ask him a question. "If you could have those same feelings back again, only on a deeper level, would you be willing to try something"? If the answer is 'yes' then I have several other questions.

The first is this. "What does your wife like for breakfast?" Some men cannot remember. "Does she like pancakes, porridge, toast, tea or coffee?" After a bit of time we usually establish what she likes. I then tell this man that for the next 30 days he is going to make his wife breakfast. Some laugh, some tell me that it's a man's job to buy flowers, not cook breakfast. At this point I remind them that if they wish to be Christlike, then they should follow Jesus' example (John 21: 9-13) and cook breakfast. Most agree to this commitment in order to save their marriage, not realizing that my intention is to set them on a path of learning the fundamentals of love.

When these couples return to see me 30 days later, they are usually holding hands. Men have shared how this simple 30 day commitment changed their lives. The first couple of days they made breakfast reluctantly. Some explained to their wives that they had made a deal with me, others did not, but wives usually thought it a novel idea and were grateful. Then something powerful begins to happen. Instead of seeking 'eros' love all the time, husbands begin to experience the practical manifestations of 'agape' love. There is a spiritual principle at work.

Through doing simple acts of love, loving feelings are generated.

They initially presumed my suggestion was just to give their wife a break, but they were wrong. When they see the joy that this simple act brings to their wives, that joy finds a place in their hearts and romantic feelings blossom once again, only this time, those feelings are grounded in servant love, the love which is the heart of Christ, the love which cannot be purchased with flowers.

At this time I am able to explain to them why it is so often that husbands 'fall out of love' rather than their wives. In this culture it is women who serve in the home, a direct form of servant love. She constantly does loving acts for her husband and children but receives little of the same in return. But, having her husband serve her out of love generates deep respect. When both partners are operating in servant/agape love, the romantic/eros love takes care of itself.

Such is Paul's command to husbands; love with agape love in the same way as Christ loves with agape love. For further study on this topic, especially regarding preparation for marriage, I would recommend reading *Unmasked: Exposing the Cultural Sexual Assault* by Jim Anderson (www.lifeline-ministries.org).

Study Eighteen

Instructions to Children

Colossians 3: 20

²⁰ Children, obey your parents in everything, for this pleases the Lord.

In this study we will examine the role of children in a Christian family, examine the cultural differences in modern and biblical cultures, and determine if these differences should affect how we view children in regards to salvation. To begin with, we need to find a biblical definition of 'child' and perhaps more importantly, what we mean by salvation.

One of the interesting anomalies of the New Testament (NT) is that the apostle Paul quotes the old covenant in the law when addressing children, a fact seen in his parallel passage in Ephesians 6: 1-4 which reads:

6 Children, obey your parents in the Lord, for this is right. ² "Honor your father and mother"—which is the first commandment with a promise— ³ "so that it may go well with you and that you may enjoy long life on the earth."

Paul believed that Christians were no longer under law, however, he makes an exception regarding Christian children. In biblical culture, children were considered to be under the spiritual authority of their parents, rather than independent of them. A child's standing with God was a reflection of his/her parents standing with God, not independent of it. In our modern cultures we have created divisions within the Church for 'child evangelism'; however, the Bible never suggests that the children of Christian parents are unsaved in the first place. Turn to 1st Corinthians 7:14.

111

¹⁴ For the unbelieving husband has been sanctified through his wife, and the unbelieving wife has been sanctified through her believing husband. Otherwise your children would be unclean, but as it is, they are holy.

In this passage of Scripture Paul is primarily addressing the issue of divorce. Some new Christians were concerned that perhaps they should divorce their unbelieving spouse. Paul tells them no. In the verse we have just read the apostle tells them that the believing spouse 'sanctifies' the marriage, meaning the marriage is holy before God. Paul is never suggesting that the unbeliever is saved, a fact he makes clear in verse 16. Paul's point is that the marriage, of which 'the two are one flesh' is sanctified, and therefore under the spiritual authority of Jesus Christ.

He then states that the children of such a marriage are 'holy'. The Greek word used is *hagios,* the same word used to describe Christian saints who have been made holy by Christ, and the Old Testament (OT) saints who resurrected after the resurrection of Christ in Matthew 27:52.

Much of the confusion surrounding this issue comes from some fundamental misunderstandings about what salvation is, and the differences between the old and new covenants. Is there, or rather, can there be a difference between 'saved' and 'born again'? I believe there is and can be, and understanding that difference sheds light on the role of children. Let's briefly see the difference between old and new covenants. The new covenant began on the Day of Pentecost. This was the first time in human history when the Holy Spirit came to dwell within believers, a day prophesied throughout the OT. The Spirit of God was upon specific people prior to this, but never within them. Hebrews 11 testifies to this, speaking about a great list of OT saints who lived by faith, and ends with these words in verses 39-40.

³⁹ These were all commended for their faith, yet none of them received what had been promised, ⁴⁰ since God had planned something better for us so that only together with us would they be made perfect.

The 'something better' is the new covenant which could only commence after a perfect sacrifice was offered for sin, namely Jesus

Christ. These OT saints never experienced new birth, for the new covenant was the outpouring of the Holy Spirit into the lives of believers. Jesus had told His disciples this very thing when speaking of the Holy Spirit, saying that *'he lives with you and will be in you'* (John 14:17). The Holy Spirit was with them during their ministry with Jesus, yet although they had already been sent out and performed miracles, when He was arrested they fled. However, after Pentecost these men were born again and filled with the Spirit and their fear dissolved; they preached fearlessly and most were martyred for their witness.

Jesus also explained all of this to Nicodemus, a godly man who visited Him. In John 3:3 Jesus tells Nicodemus that unless he is born again he cannot 'see' the kingdom of heaven. The tense of this verb *'horao'* means to receive and experience *now*, while we are still alive. When we are born again the Kingdom of Heaven comes to reside in us, we sense its presence in the indwelling Divine Nature. These, then are the differences between the old and new covenants, therefore, we can make some conclusions.

Were David, Abraham, Moses and the other OT saints born again? No, they were not, for Christ had not been sacrificed for sin. Were they saved? Absolutely yes, for David spoke of his salvation and Christ spoke of Abraham in heaven in His discourse about the rich man and Lazarus (Luke 16:23).

Understanding this distinction is vital to correctly interpreting God's command to Christian children. They are 'holy' as the OT saints were holy, and in as much as they obey God's command to obey their parents, they are 'saved' in the same way as the OT saints are saved under the old covenant.

The question remains, then, when does a child cease to be a child? This is a more complex issue because many believe that cultural differences must influence the answer. On top of this there is the problem of how the gospel is presented. As I have stated in earlier studies, and outlined in detail in my book *'Running the Race',* being born again is about a total surrender of an individual's will and ego to the will of God in Christ. We are called to 'make disciples', not weak converts, and salvation is about receiving Christ as Lord (Colossians 2:6), not merely believing about Him as Savior.

In our modern cultures we use the term 'age of understanding' to give a license to preach hell-fire to children, but the Bible has no such term or concept. In Scripture, God defines children by an 'age of independence', a time when He considers that a person is independent of their parents and, therefore, able to give their lives to Him.

This idea is clearly illustrated in the story of the Exodus in Numbers 14:29-31. The Jews had been brought out of Egypt with demonstrations of God's power. They had seen the plagues, walked through the Red Sea, heard God at Mount Sinai and received the Commandments; they had been fed with manna and supplied with water from a rock, but when they heard the report of the spies about the Nephilim they refused to trust God. In His anger the Lord was going to destroy them all and start afresh with Moses. Moses talked Him out of this, but God swore that no person twenty years old and over would ever enter the Promised Land. Those nineteen and younger spent forty years in the desert until all of the others died, and then they had their opportunity to trust the Lord under the command of Joshua.

On this occasion God decided that those under twenty were not old enough, or independent enough, to make a life or death decision about trusting Him. This gives us an insight into God's view of maturity and salvation. Obviously there would have been children who were more independent than others, but He drew a line at twenty. Also, there would have been teenagers who were under twenty who were more spiritually mature than others, and possibly even teens who wanted to trust God as Joshua and Caleb did. We don't know if this was the case or not, but God drew a line at twenty for reasons known only to Him.

If we were to be legalistic, we could state that God sees all persons under twenty years old as children, but this would be foolish for it is not the intention of the passage. Therefore, taking all of the passages we have studied into account, we need to come to a wise decision about what is expected of especially teens.

Being a teen is one of the most difficult times of a person's life. You're neither a child nor an adult. At fifteen you're old enough to produce children, but not old enough to bear the responsibility of being a parent. With hormones surging through your body, and natural drives calling you to learn to be an independent person, it can be very confusing. Then of course there's peer pressure, curiosity, and other factors. Most of us make some of our silliest mistakes when we're teens, and we need strong, understanding parents who can hold the

114

end of the line, give us enough rope to explore life and even make a few mistakes, yet stop us from driving ourselves over a cliff.

God understands this time in a person's life, and He often allows us to go through difficulties to teach us how much we really need Him. Unfortunately, many Christian parents push their teens into making a commitment during these very turbulent years, simply to try and save themselves the pain of parenting. Youth pastors end up becoming teenage babysitters who are expected to rush teens into 'making a decision' in the hope that they will suddenly become model adult Christians. Sadly, many teens who have tried smoking, or had alcohol against their parents commands, or played around with sexual activities, come under conviction and rightfully repent, only to be told that they are now 'born again'.

Is God not allowed to convict a teen to repent of simply disobeying his/her parents? Does repentance always mean that the next moment must be the 'born again' moment? Is God not allowed to see this repentant teen as 'saved' and call them to surrender their entire lives at a time He considers right? I have witnessed countless teens who repented of something at fifteen, were told they were 'born again', and almost immediately fell away. Many come back to Christ when He calls them at a later date and are born again, and go on to live their lives for Him. Yet there are others who never return, for they are convinced that they have 'been there, done that' and Christianity has no power to change the human heart.

I sincerely believe that no person has the right to tell another they are born again and filled with the Spirit. Surely, if this experience has occurred, the person will know? I went forward in an evangelical meeting and repented at fifteen after my friend was killed in a car accident. I burned my girly magazines, left the heavy rock band, gave up smoking and tried to live the Christian life. I tried to read the Bible but couldn't understand the epistles at all. The gospels were great stories, but those letters written to the Church could only be understood by the indwelling Spirit, and He wasn't living in me, even though the pastor told me I was born again. He was wrong. My 'conversion' lasted three months. I went back to the band, martial arts and started seeking an answer to life outside of Christianity, for I was convinced it had no power to change me.

God called me ten years later and I was born again. I needed no man to tell me, indeed, I was alone in my room at the time. That day I surrendered all to His command, I fell in love with Him, and the Scriptures were as alive as if they were within me. The interpreter had taken up residence permanently.

What then is the role of a child and teenager? Simply this: to obey their parents as unto the Lord, learn to trust God and build faith in Him, so that when He calls them to surrender their lives to Him completely, they will be ready. This will mean repentance, mistakes, and more repentance and mistakes, and God, like in the Exodus, will be leading through the Sea, showing Himself, teaching faith and His commands, until He brings this person to the banks of the river. At that time there will be a challenge, perhaps a mighty and fearful challenge, that which we could call 'counting the cost', and God's call will be an all and everything call. God calls us to give Him our lives when He decides our lives are ours to give, not before.

And what is a parent's role? To teach their child to trust God and have faith in Him, to repent when they make mistakes, and to tell their child that one day, in His perfect time, God will call them to surrender their entire lives to Him, a day He chooses, a day that He considers them spiritually independent of their parents.

And the role of youth leaders? To support parents in preparing teens for that day, not pushing children that God considers 'saved' into a pseudo born again experience, as if we had the right to decide when that should be. Let God be God. Remember, that God sent John the Baptist with a ministry of baptism for repentance to prepare people for the coming of Christ. Teaching a child or teen to repent is simply part of the training we need before coming to Christ. It only means to turn back and face God, not that we are continually saved and lost, saved and lost again as some teach.

As for the topic of the children and teens of unbelieving parents, I have little to say, for the Bible hardly touches on this subject specifically. However, there are several passages which strongly suggest that they are under their parent's spiritual authority, even if that authority is against the teachings of Scripture. The children of false prophets sometimes shared the same fate as their parents; however, our God is just and calls all to turn to Him.

And finally a few words about the Biblical term 'household'. Some Christians quote Acts 11:14 where Peter told Cornelius that he and all his household would be saved, meaning that children can be born again. Two points to be made here. Firstly, Peter was most likely

116

referring to the slaves and servants of a household, rather than the children. But, in any case, Paul's theology was that if any one of the parents was born again, then the children automatically came under that spiritual authority and were considered 'holy', saved under the old covenant. There are similar passages in Acts 16:15, 16:31, 18:8. These Scriptures cannot be used to contradict God's blatant commandment for children to obey their parents as unto the Lord. In this sense, the parents are Lord and master, until He takes that place in His perfect time.

For further thoughts on the topic of Biblical salvation, please read chapter one of *Running the Race*.

Study Nineteen

Slavery

Colossians 3:22-4:1

²² Slaves, obey your earthly masters in everything; and do it, not only when their eye is on you and to curry their favor, but with sincerity of heart and reverence for the Lord. ²³ Whatever you do, work at it with all your heart, as working for the Lord, not for human masters, ²⁴ since you know that you will receive an inheritance from the Lord as a reward. It is the Lord Christ you are serving. ²⁵ Anyone who does wrong will be repaid for their wrongs, and there is no favoritism. 4 Masters, provide your slaves with what is right and fair, because you know that you also have a Master in heaven.

The Roman jurist Gaius once wrote that:

"Slavery is a human invention and not found in nature. Indeed, it was that other human invention, war, which provided the bulk of slaves, but they were also the bounty of piracy ... or the product of breeding."

To the modern mind slavery is something to be condemned and abolished in all its forms, yet it has been a part of human cultures for thousands of years and still exists today in even more diabolical ways than in the 1st Century or Atlantic Slave Trade of more recent times. Although almost all modern governments have made slavery illegal, practices such as bonded labor, where a person's work is the security for a debt, are rampant in poor countries. It is estimated that in India alone, around 15 million children are bonded laborers, having been 'sold' to employers to pay off family debt. The salaries are so low, and costs of living so high, that many remain in this situation for life. On top of this there is the practice of forced marriages, selling daughters when the dowry is too small, forced prostitution (sex trafficking), children forced into armies, etc.

Apart from the above, there are also many other forms of physical and mental slavery which dominate the lives of people in 1st World cultures, such as drug and alcohol addictions, greed, lust and a host of others. A man may be flying above the clouds in his private jet and still be a slave to the desires, guilt and greed which dominate his life. Slavery, then, is not a simple topic to be dismissed lightly, for it can affect people in every walk of life. The issue of slavery and its eradication is found only in the annihilation of the sin principle which has enslaved every person since the fall of humanity in the Garden of Eden.

Such is the priority of the Bible, not the changing of government policies or cultures, but the transformation of the human heart into the freedom from sin which can only be found in Jesus Christ. History has shown that where true Christianity has become a major influence within cultures, those cultures have been transformed. The abolition of slavery in Great Britain during the Great Awakenings is a good example; however, sadly, the Bible has also been abused and twisted to condone slavery as in pre-civil war America.

In Old Testament times slavery was commonly tied to the spoils of war. When kings invaded and conquered their rivals, slavery was imposed to control the conquered population and drive the economy. With the Israelites this situation had a slightly different view. The Hebrews were not allowed to enslave fellow Hebrews (Jeremiah 34:8-9, Leviticus 25:42) although this command was often disobeyed. Also, God used the slave cultures of the nations around Israel to teach and punish His chosen people.

By the time of the Roman Empire slavery was an integral part of the culture of the known world. There was a great deal of cruelty, and even several uprisings, which eventually began to change the attitudes within Roman culture. The Romans had a great deal of laws concerning slaves, laws which were often amended to include slave's rights. As Christianity took hold in the empire these laws eventually included land ownership rights and even the right to vote.

The New Testament writers never address slavery as something which needs to be abolished, perhaps for several reasons. Firstly, most of the apostles, as far as we can see, believed that the return of Christ was imminent. See for example 1st Corinthians 7: 29, James 5:8. The apostle's main concern was to convert and prepare individuals for the coming of Christ. Secondly, the apostles taught that every government institution was ultimately under the control of God and, therefore, did not encourage Christians to get involved in politics. Thirdly, the NT considers Christians to be aliens and sojourners, a people who do not belong to this world but are citizens of heaven as Paul tells us in Philippians 3: 20-21.

20 But our citizenship is in heaven. And we eagerly await a Savior from there, the Lord Jesus Christ, 21 who, by the power that enables him to bring everything under his control, will transform our lowly bodies so that they will be like his glorious body.

Therefore, what we find in Paul's instructions to slaves and masters is the application of eternal values to the position each individual is in. Paul is not concerned to change our station in life, but rather to encourage every Christian, slave or free, to serve as if serving Christ. In other words, Christian mentality is in many ways a slave/servant mentality. Jesus taught this very thing when speaking to His disciples about greatness. In Mark 10:44 he says that 'whoever wants to be first must be the slave of all'.

Paul encourages slaves to '*obey your earthly masters in everything; and do it, not only when their eye is on you and to curry their favor, but with sincerity of heart and reverence for the Lord. 23 Whatever you do, work at it with all your heart, as working for the Lord, not for human masters, 24 since you know that you will receive an inheritance from the Lord as a reward. It is the Lord Christ you are serving.*

To the secular mind these instructions may seem to condone the evils of considering human beings as property, but the NT understanding is that every Christian is the 'possession of God' (Ephesians 1:14), we are people who 'belong to Christ' (Romans 8:9). This is the heart of salvation; that we surrender our wills to the will of God, giving up our rights, and in turn, inheriting the right to be called God's children. No matter our station in life we are to live as to Christ, looking at our status as children of God and the inheritance that we are entitled to in Him. Whether we are elders, pastors, husbands, wives, slaves or freemen, it is the Lord we are serving, and our heavenly reward will reflect our 'sincerity of heart and reverence' for Him. To the owners of slaves Paul had words of warning which reflect exactly what we have just discussed.

4 Masters, provide your slaves with what is right and fair, because you know that you also have a Master in heaven.

Masters are commanded to treat those under their authority in the knowledge that they are under the same authority, namely Christ. In Ephesians 6, Paul makes his point even clearer.

5 Slaves, obey your earthly masters with respect and fear, and with sincerity of heart, just as you would obey Christ. 6 Obey them not only to win their favor when their eye is on you, but as slaves of Christ, doing the will of God from your heart.

7 Serve wholeheartedly, as if you were serving the Lord, not people, 8 because you know that the Lord will reward each one for whatever good they do, whether they are slave or free.

9 And masters, treat your slaves in the same way. Do not threaten them, since you know that he who is both their Master and yours is in heaven, and there is no favoritism with him.

Masters are commanded to understand that their heavenly reward will reflect how Christlike they were in treating those under their authority and possession. It is difficult for us to fully comprehend the cultural attitudes towards slavery in the 1st Century. When we are born into a particular culture we intend to see it as a norm and accept it. However, history also records times when Christian revivals have been the catalyst for the abolition of slavery, such as during the Great Awakening which witnessed the abolition of child slavery during the industrial revolution in Great Britain, and the Civil War in America. The primary role of the Holy Spirit at such times was not revolution, or the reformation of cultures, but rather regeneration. The principle at work here is that when the human heart if transformed, cultures are also transformed.

Those who criticize the Bible often point to the fact that Jesus and His apostles never condemn slavery, however, these people fail to understand the fundamental principle which the Bible points to, namely, that all human beings are slaves. In John 8:34 Jesus said that 'whoever sins is a slave to sin' and that 'if the Son sets you free you will be free indeed'. The apostle Paul has much to say to Christians on this topic, especially in Romans chapters 6-8. In chapter six Paul outlines our spiritual position if, indeed, we are truly in Christ.

6 What shall we say, then? Shall we go on sinning so that grace may increase? ² By no means! We are those who have died to sin; how can we live in it any longer? ³ Or don't you know that all of us who were baptized into Christ Jesus were baptized into his death? ⁴ We were therefore buried with him through baptism into death in order that, just as Christ was raised from the dead through the glory of the Father, we too may live a new life.

⁵ For if we have been united with him in a death like his, we will certainly also be united with him in a resurrection like his. ⁶ For we know that our old self was crucified with him so that the body ruled by sin might be done away with, that we should no longer be slaves to sin— ⁷ because anyone who has died has been set free from sin.

⁸ Now if we died with Christ, we believe that we will also live with him. ⁹ For we know that since Christ was raised from the dead, he cannot die again; death no longer has mastery over him. ¹⁰ The death he died, he died to sin once for all; but the life he lives, he lives to God.

¹¹ In the same way, count yourselves dead to sin but alive to God in Christ Jesus. ¹² Therefore do not let sin reign in your mortal body so that you obey its evil desires. ¹³ Do not offer any part of yourself to sin as an instrument of wickedness, but rather offer yourselves to God as those who have been brought from death to life; and offer every part of yourself to him as an instrument of righteousness. ¹⁴ For sin shall no longer be your master, because you are not under the law, but under grace.

In this passage Paul's argument is that regeneration means we have died with Christ and been united with Him in His death. The 'old self' he refers to is the rebellious ego which demanded to rule in the individual and remain a slave to sin. If we have surrendered our wills to the will of God, this ego has been 'crucified with Christ' and, therefore, 'freed from sin'. Please notice again that Paul uses the conditional 'if' in verse 8. That little word 'if' literally shouts at the reader to examine themselves to make a conclusion about how genuine their regeneration is. Paul also challenges us about the daily decisions we make, challenging us about what we 'offer' our bodies to, and in 12:1-2 he concludes this thought with the following words.

12 Therefore, I urge you, brothers and sisters, in view of God's mercy, to offer your bodies as a living sacrifice, holy and pleasing to God—this is your true and proper worship. ² Do not conform to the pattern of this world, but be transformed by the renewing of your mind. Then you will be able to test and approve what God's will is— his good, pleasing and perfect will.

The key verb in these verses is 'offer'. This is a conscious action of the will, and oftentimes a mental and spiritual battle. Our sin nature tries to seduce us to offer our bodies to sin, but the Holy Spirit calls us to deny our sin nature and offer our bodies to righteousness. Christians retain the old nature after they have received the Divine Nature. The driving force of the old nature, the ego, has been crucified with Christ, but the habits and desires of that nature still desire to sin, whilst the Divine Nature calls us daily to holiness. Our free will is not destroyed when we give our lives to Christ, rather, it is united to another will, the will of our Holy Lord who leads us to live for Him.

I encourage you to take the time to read Romans 6-8. Paul uses the language of slavery predominately in chapter 6, but in a positive way. We have become slaves to righteousness, slaves to holiness, but this form of slavery is the heart of true freedom. Therein lies the wonderful paradox of being born again. We submit our wills completely to the will of God, becoming bonded slaves to His will, and in doing so, receive the freedom from our slavery to sin that is found in the holiness of Jesus Christ. This is Paul's message in chapter 8, a message of encouragement that we now 'belong to Christ' (v9) and have 'no obligation to our sinful natures'. In verse 13 he tells us that it is 'by the Spirit' that we can put to death the misdeeds of our bodies, and in verses 15-16, that we no longer need to be slaves to fear because we are God's children.

In Summary

Slavery, in all its forms, is rooted in the fallen human nature, whether a desire to control other people for our own gain, or being controlled by our own sinful desires. The New Testament approaches the issue of slavery on two fronts. Firstly, that those who were owned by others should keep their eyes fixed on the temporary nature of this life and serve as if they are serving Jesus Christ. Likewise, their masters should be aware that God will judge them.

Secondly, that every person is born with a fallen nature which leads them to become slaves to sin. This is what we might call 'primary slavery', and without emancipation through being born again, this form of slavery is eternal. If through faith we are set free by Christ, then we are free indeed, for nothing can separate us from the love of God, and furthermore, the indwelling Spirit of God motivates and empowers us to live our lives free from the bondage of sin.

Study Twenty

Final Instructions

Colossians 4: 2-6, 7-18

2 Devote yourselves to prayer, being watchful and thankful. 3 And pray for us, too, that God may open a door for our message, so that we may proclaim the mystery of Christ, for which I am in chains. 4 Pray that I may proclaim it clearly, as I should. 5 Be wise in the way you act toward outsiders; make the most of every opportunity. 6 Let your conversation be always full of grace, seasoned with salt, so that you may know how to answer everyone.

In this passage Paul offers his final instructions to the Churches in and around Colossae. As in many other letters, (Romans 12:12, Ephesians 6:18, Philippians 4:6) he urges them to be intercessors in the work of the gospel, both for themselves and for he and other leaders who are working as missionaries. Let's take a look at some of the key words in this passage.

'Devote yourselves to prayer'

Devotion to prayer is a great challenge to all of us and something I believe that most Christians struggle with, including me. The word Paul uses is *'prostakerio'* which means to attend to something constantly. Many of us live very busy lives, working long hours and often bringing our work home with us. After spending 8-10 hours each day at work, driving home, trying to spend time with family and getting a chance to put our feet up and relax, often the last thing on our minds is to go into a room and spend an hour interceding on our knees. Others spend countless hours on social media sites, watching TV, playing sports, and then there are often the many meetings connected to Church activities we may be involved in.

How then are we to attend to prayer constantly?

125

Some Christians are early risers and have established the habit of having a 'quiet time' before they start their day. Others are 'night owls' who struggle to get out of bed and don't have a set time for prayer. We are all different, and our circumstances often dictate when and where we can devote time to prayer. What Paul is telling us here is to find that time and make it a priority, rather than it being the last thing on our daily list of appointments. Personally, I don't think the Lord minds if our prayer time is spent on the mountaintop, in a quiet room, or walking the dog. If the only time you can get alone with God is when you're walking your dog, then make this your prayer time, but find that time and keep it for Him.

Having said that, Paul also has in mind his desire that we 'pray without ceasing', as he writes in 1st Thessalonians 5:17. I believe that this idea is often misunderstood and can be an area of condemnation and discouragement. I well remember as a young Christian reading the words of A.W Tozer who spoke about 'practicing the presence of God'. Here is a small exert on this topic from my book *Running the Race*.

'This idea of practicing the presence of God has been a great blessing to me over the years. Tozer was referring to the fact that Christ is always with us, both within and without - the presence of the Holy Spirit within us, and the fact that Christ walks with us every moment of the day.

Fundamentally, prayer is communication with God, but communication doesn't necessarily mean that I must stop what I'm doing, get on my knees, and make petitions about everything. For about 30 years I have practiced the presence of God, meaning simply that I go through my day knowing I am never alone. Often I speak out loud and have been accused by some - in both amusing and mocking tones - that I have 'an imaginary friend'. I have an *invisible* friend, but He is certainly not imaginary. I talk to my Lord all day. I try to be wise about when I speak out loud as some would be calling those 'nice young men in long white coats to come and take me away'. My wife is used to it.

There are many times when I get on my knees and make petitions and requests, or simply give adoration and homage to my Holy Lord, and for me, singing songs is also a form of prayer. But living the

126

Christian life in the knowledge that Jesus Christ is always beside me has been the greatest help to me for sanctification, of which prayer is an enormous part. Too many Christians get the idea that when they finish praying, it's as though they have walked out of God's room and closed the door. It's too easy to give in to temptation if we fool ourselves into believing that the Lord's head is turned the other way, but when we live constantly in the knowledge that He is always with us, it is as though we have a chaperone helping us in every situation'.

Devoting ourselves to prayer doesn't need to feel like an odious task. Begin to practice the presence of God every day, and, in essence you will be 'attending to prayer constantly'.

'Watchful'

Paul mentions being watchful and thankful. In the context of Colossians his warning to watchfulness is closely tied to what he has been saying throughout the letter about false doctrines, and is a warning to us also. The warning is reminiscent of the 'watcher on the wall', the soldier who takes the responsibility to look out for an attacking enemy. Time was divided into watches, usually of about four hours each and then the guard was changed. The Colossians, and we, are called to guard the walls, to ensure that the enemy does not sneak into the Church to bring discord and destruction through false teaching. Jesus also used this word frequently in warning people to be watching for the signs of His coming (Matthew 24: 42, 25:13) and perhaps Paul has this in mind also

'Thankful'

In chapter 1:12 Paul tells us we should be *'joyfully giving thanks to the Father, who has qualified you to share in the inheritance of the saints in the kingdom of light'*. There is nothing more important in a Christian's life than gratitude to God. Gratitude expresses humility and humility is the key to the heart of God. So many Christians get so immersed in the busyness of their lives that they take their eyes off the inheritance we have been given as 'co-heirs with Christ'. The world drags our gaze downwards, but God's purpose is to prepare us for the heavenly kingdom of which we have been given a taste.

Being thankful directs our focus on the cross and heavenward. In times of difficulty thankfulness expresses our willingness to trust the Lord, to trust Him because He has been trustworthy throughout similar times we have experienced. Live in an attitude of thankfulness, for as His children, such an attitude delights the heart of God.

'May open a door'

In verse 3 Paul asks the Colossians to pray that God might open a door for him and his fellow prisoners to preach the mystery of Christ. Some scholars believe that he is asking them to pray for his release, and he may have this in mind, however, from a close reading of Acts 28 we can see that Paul spoke boldly to those who visited him while he was under house arrest in Rome. It is more likely, then, that the apostle is seeking courage to continue preaching the gospel, knowing that the consequences might be his death. Whatever the case, it is obvious that Paul understood that every opportunity to preach was given by the Lord 'opening a door', and also that, although he had preached the mystery of Christ countless times, he always relied on Christ to give him the right words for every occasion. He expresses this same idea in Ephesians 6:19 where he writes, *'pray also for me, that whenever I open my mouth, words may be given me so that I will fearlessly make known the mystery of the gospel'.*

Outsiders

⁵ Be wise in the way you act toward outsiders; make the most of every opportunity. ⁶ Let your conversation be always full of grace, seasoned with salt, so that you may know how to answer everyone.

In these verses Paul has obviously shifted his focus away from the immediate problem of Gnosticism within the Church, and is calling on the Colossians to take hold of the message within the letter and look outward. Paul calls on his readers to use wisdom when acting toward and speaking to 'outsiders'. The phrase 'seasoned with salt' also refers to using wisdom, a common idiom and analogy used in the 1st Century. He calls us to make the most of every opportunity, but only through the application of grace towards unbelievers we speak to, and to use wisdom, for wisdom rightly applied knows how to answer. There are several important lessons for us in these instructions.

Firstly, to make the most of every opportunity. Notice please that Paul uses the word wisdom before speaking of making the most of opportunities. Oftentimes, a kind act, a loving embrace and sympathetic shoulder are more powerful than our words. Wisdom knows when to be silent and when to speak. We are called to be 'led by the Holy Spirit', to listen to His voice and obey when He prompts us to speak. Sometimes that will take courage, but know that the Lord will give us the right words to say.

Secondly, that our conversation 'be always full of grace'. Of all people, Christians should be the ones who understand what it is to have received grace, yet too often we are the least likely to apply it to others. Many Churches unconsciously adopt an 'us and them' mentality towards unbelievers which creates a dividing wall. I have found this attitude most prominent in those who have never stepped out of the relative safety of the Christian cultures in which they were raised. Homeschooling, Christian universities, and the like, may be well-intentioned, but sadly, they can also contribute to an attitude which exudes self-righteousness, if an 'us and them' mentality is adopted.

The well-known parable of the prodigal son (Luke 15) is a good example of Jesus attitude towards the self-righteous. Whilst one son had followed his fallen nature and indulged himself in every sin imaginable, the other had stayed at home, albeit, somewhat grudgingly. Jesus was speaking to a group of Pharisees at the time and His point was never that it's better to go out and sin in order to know you're a sinner, but rather, that seeing yourself as righteous could push you further from grace than the most vile. The woman who entered Simon the Pharisee's home and wept on Jesus feet, received grace, whilst at the same time Simon condemned her. Romans 3:23 reminds us that 'all have sinned and fall short of the glory of God', and therefore, all require the grace of God to be saved.

Thirdly, Paul tells us that if our conversations are full of grace and seasoned with wisdom, then we will know how to answer everyone. A person who is full of grace is one who lives in an attitude of humility, and such is wisdom before God. Proverbs 11: 2 says that 'with pride comes disgrace, but with humility comes wisdom'. Pride brings disgrace upon the gospel, for the proud have lost touch with the fact that they were hopelessly lost without the grace of God. When such people attempt to engage unbelievers in conversation, the result is seldom, if ever, positive, indeed usually the unbeliever feels attacked and justified in rejecting the message. We are called to get alongside people, to serve them, and in this way to imitate the humility and wisdom of Christ.

The verses we have looked at in this study end Paul's instructions to the Churches in and around Colossae. In the final part of chapter four he speaks about his circumstances and sends greetings from various leaders who are working with him, including Epaphras who had brought the report to Rome. He gives a personal recommendation about Epaphras, greets the brothers at Laodicea, and a woman called Nympha who has a congregation in her house. He asks them to 'remember his chains', a request for prayers, and closes with a blessing of grace over them.

In Summary

The letter to the Colossians has one primary and foundational message; namely, that Jesus Christ is the beginning and the end, the Creator and Sustainer of all things, the one who reconciles us to the Godhead through His sacrifice on the cross, who unites us with Him in His death and resurrection, who is the mystery revealed, the One in whom we are hidden, the One in whom the fullness of Deity lives in bodily form, and that we have been given fullness in Him. The answer to every question is found in Jesus Christ, for in Him are hidden all the treasures of wisdom and knowledge.

And finally, through Christ, we who were once dead have been made alive; we have been freed from human traditions and deceptive philosophies, have become God's chosen people, holy and dearly loved, are called to forgive as we were forgiven, to clothe ourselves with love, and do all in the name of the Lord Jesus, giving thanks to the Father through Him.

My prayer is that these studies have been a blessing and encouragement to you. God bless, and grace be with you.

Also by Steve Copland

Mary Magdalene: A Woman Who Loved

1st Century Trilogy - Book One

Throughout history there has been much written about Mary of Magdala, most of it legend and speculation, some of it derogatory. The Bible, however, gives us many clues as to the character, personality and contributions this first century woman made to the ministry of Christ and the early church. This book is, in many ways, a tribute to a woman whose life was dramatically changed by the one she came to love more than life itself.

Mary Magdalene was a woman whose life circumstances led her from demonic possession and prostitution to being the first witness of the greatest event in world history. In an attempt to reconstruct her life, this book demonstrates her struggle as she confronts the patriarchal traditions embedded in first century culture, the hypocritical practice of condemning only one gender in adultery, her transformation as she finds grace, freedom and real love in her encounter with Christ, and her being chosen as 'the apostle to the apostles'.

This novel takes the reader into the first century. It delves into the personal lives of lepers, cripples and the sight impaired; it goes on a journey from the battlefields of ancient Germania to Jerusalem with two Roman soldiers who end up initiated into the cult of Mithraism; it explores the fears, prejudices and arrogance of the religious rulers of Israel, and the ambitions of Judas Iscariot; it portrays the everyday struggles of first century people in an occupied land; it looks behind the scenes at a woman who is seduced into committing adultery and used to test Jesus, and brings them all together beneath the cross of Jesus Christ.

Simon and Simon: Passion and Power

1st Century Trilogy - Book Two

Simon and Simon is the second novel of the 1st century trilogy. It features two men born just a few miles apart whose lives are

131

dramatically different, Simon Peter and Simon Magus. Simon Peter's life weaves through the story and is contrasted with Magus, the one known as 'Simon the Sorcerer'. The latter travels to Kashmir and studies the Rig Veda in search of individual power. He returns to Israel where he meets Simon Peter. Both end up in Rome: one levitates for Nero, the other is crucified. Triarius is a Roman soldier married for only a few months and sent to the Northern frontier. His wife is pregnant when he leaves and believed to be carrying a son, if the witch was correct. He sends orders to dispose of the child if the hag is mistaken. His wife gives birth to a daughter, 'Triaria', and secretly raises the child while her husband is away, not knowing if he will return. He does, and discovers the child's existence, and...well that would be telling the story.

Religion: History and Mystery

War, Power, Greed, Jihad, Inquisition, Crusades and Extremists, all words we associate with religion. Shamans, priests, prophets and magicians, servants of the gods, mediums of power, or frauds? 22 religions, examined, exposed and deciphered.

Religion: History and Mystery explores the ancient and modern religions which have dominated the world for 6000 years, exposes the contradictions, uncovers the mysteries, and reveals the truth of who and what we are. This book also points out why Judaism and Christianity are so incredibly distinct from every other religion. Is there a Divine Mystery contained in the Bible which is absent in all other religious texts?

Running the Race

Every generation of Christians face challenges in 'running the race of faith'. Living for Christ in the 21st Century is no exception. The Apostle Paul warned that 'the time will come when men will not put up with sound doctrine. Instead, to suit their own desires, they will gather around them a great number of teachers to say what their itching ears want to hear'. We are living in such times. We should not be surprised, for Jesus warned us there would be many false prophets in the Last Days before His return.

'Running the Race' challenges the extremes, throws light on the shadows, and illuminates the path which Christ has set before those who have trusted Him with their lives.

Slug: The Reluctant Butterfly

Slug wants to fly, but he doesn't want to die. Slug is a beautiful story about our reluctance to allow God to transform us into what He wants us to become. Slug learns through his mistakes that many will lead us down wrong paths, but obedience to our Creator brings complete joy and fulfillment. Grunt, a crow and central character in the story, discovers the pitfalls of peer pressure, the power of forgiveness, and eventual self acceptance in his new life. (Children ages 7-11)

Time for Truth: A Challenge to Skeptics

Time for truth challenges skeptics to take a fresh look at the supernatural qualities of the Bible. Issues such as the existence of God, creation/evolution, evil and suffering are discussed, and the reader is taken on a logical, scientific and inspiring walk through world history as a story of God's plan for humanity. This book has been used in various forms since 1985 when it was first written for a man dying of cancer. He refused to speak of God. He was an ardent atheist; however, he had a spiritual transformation just three days before he died and witnessed of his faith in Christ.

Perfection

Within the human soul a voice calls us to reach for perfection. In every area of our lives we demonstrate a desire to know, experience and create that which is perfect. The clothes we wear, the flowers we choose, religions we practice and love we seek, all testify to our instinct to reject that which we perceive as flawed, and strive for beauty, contentment and fulfillment. Is it possible for us to know and experience perfection? The answer is 'yes'.

Just Because: The Story of Salvation for Children

Just Because takes children on an exciting and inspirational journey through the Bible. It gives them an exciting bird's-eye-view of God's plan unfolding as He prepares the world for the coming of Jesus Christ. Throughout the story Satan is watching out for the child who will "crush his head," (Genesis 3) and he endeavors to stop God's plan from unfolding. The reader knows who that special child is, and the story especially opens up the insights that point to Jesus throughout the Old Testament. Each chapter takes about twenty minutes to read and ends with a short Biblical lesson. Children love it.

Contact details for conference, seminar and book enquiries.

http://www.stevecopland.com
copland56@yahoo.co.nz
Facebook: Steve Copland
New Life Church Kiev Ukraine

CPSIA information can be obtained
at www.ICGtesting.com
Printed in the USA
FSHW021254041220
76590FS

9 781502 909671